First World War
and Army of Occupation
War Diary
France, Belgium and Germany

40 DIVISION
Divisional Troops
Worcestershire Regiment
17th Battalion Pioneers
1 May 1918 - 8 October 1919

WO95/2601/4

The Naval & Military Press Ltd
www.nmarchive.com
Published in association with The National Archives

Published by

The Naval & Military Press Ltd

Unit 10 Ridgewood Industrial Park,

Uckfield, East Sussex,

TN22 5QE England

Tel: +44 (0) 1825 749494

www.naval-military-press.com

www.nmarchive.com

This diary has been reprinted in facsimile from the original. Any imperfections are inevitably reproduced and the quality may fall short of modern type and cartographic standards.

© **Crown Copyright**
Images reproduced by permission of The National Archives, London, England, 2015.

Contents

Document type	Place/Title	Date From	Date To
Heading	WO95/2601/4		
Heading	17th Bn Worcestershire Regt (Pioneers) May 1918 1919 Oct		
Heading	War Diary Of 1st From G G Battn 17th G Bath Worcs Regts From May 1st 1918 May 31st 1918		
War Diary		01/05/1918	31/05/1918
Miscellaneous	Appendix I		
Miscellaneous	Appendix I Northern Sector,	27/04/1918	27/04/1918
Miscellaneous	Appendix II	24/05/1918	24/05/1918
Miscellaneous	1st Provisional Garrison Guard Battalion Operation Order No. 2	20/05/1918	20/05/1918
Miscellaneous	Appendix II		
Miscellaneous	17th Garr Battn. Worcestershire Regiment		
Miscellaneous	Standing Orders When At Rest.		
Miscellaneous	Orders For The Drevention Of Fires		
Miscellaneous	Notes Guard Mounting		
Miscellaneous	Appendix II		
Miscellaneous	Battalion Company	31/05/1918	31/05/1918
Miscellaneous	Battalion Company	30/05/1918	30/05/1918
Miscellaneous	Battalion Company	29/05/1918	29/05/1918
Miscellaneous	Battalion Company	28/05/1918	28/05/1918
Miscellaneous	Appendix III		
Miscellaneous	Medical		
Miscellaneous	Garrison Guard Brigade Training Programme	27/04/1918	27/04/1918
Miscellaneous		25/05/1918	25/05/1918
Miscellaneous	1st Prov G.G. Bn	25/05/1918	25/05/1918
Miscellaneous	17th Gn. Bn Worc Regt	27/05/1918	27/05/1918
Operation(al) Order(s)	Operation Order No 1	19/05/1918	19/05/1918
Miscellaneous	General Instructions For The Defence Of The Hauteville Sector Appendix II		
War Diary		01/06/1918	17/06/1918
War Diary	Asaline	14/06/1918	17/06/1918
War Diary	As Above On March Saiferwick Br Gn Stree 27a S.E. R.21.c 7.0	18/06/1918	21/06/1918
War Diary	Sheet 27a SE R. 21.c.7.0.	22/06/1918	22/06/1918
War Diary	On Mach O.26.d.4.7	23/06/1918	23/06/1918
War Diary	U.26.d.4.7	24/06/1918	24/06/1918
War Diary	Asalni	25/06/1918	27/06/1918
War Diary	Sheet 27 R.S.E.U 26.d. 4.7. Le Noir Trov	28/06/1918	30/06/1918
Miscellaneous	7th Bn Worcestershire Regt. Appendix VIII	29/06/1918	29/06/1918
Miscellaneous	17th G. Bn. Worcs. Regt.	05/06/1918	05/06/1918
Miscellaneous	Appendix 2 176th Infantry Brigade Order No. 112	17/06/1918	17/06/1918
Miscellaneous	Appendix III 17th Garr. Battn. Worcestershire Regt.	17/06/1918	17/06/1918
Miscellaneous			
Miscellaneous	121st Infantry Brigade Order No 20	22/06/1918	22/06/1918
Miscellaneous	Table "A" to accompany 121st Infantry Brigade Order No. 20		
Miscellaneous		23/06/1918	23/06/1918
Miscellaneous	17th Garr. Battn Worcestershire Regiment Appendix V	22/06/1918	22/06/1918
Miscellaneous	17th Garr. Battn Worcestershire Regiment Appendix V	23/06/1918	23/06/1918

Miscellaneous	Officer Commanding	24/06/1918	24/06/1918
Miscellaneous	Appendix VII		
Miscellaneous	12th Battalion Yorkshire Regiment Appendix VII		
Miscellaneous	Headquarters (a) 40th Division	02/08/1918	02/08/1918
War Diary	Sheet 27.A.S.E. U. 26. d 4.7 LE Noir Trou	01/07/1918	17/07/1918
War Diary	Sheet 27A S E U.26.D.4.7	18/07/1918	31/07/1918
Miscellaneous	Headquarter 40th Division	07/09/1918	07/09/1918
War Diary	Sheets 27 A S.E. 6.26. d. 4.7 LE Noir Trou	01/08/1918	02/08/1918
War Diary	La Belle Hotesse Sheet 36 R. C. 14.d.8.2	03/08/1918	06/08/1918
War Diary	19 Stlle Hotesse Sheet 38 A S 21.a 6.5	06/08/1918	09/08/1918
War Diary	A Belle Hotesse C.21.a.b.s.	10/08/1918	24/08/1918
War Diary	D2 C. 9.1. Sheet 36.a N.E. 1/20,000	25/08/1918	27/08/1918
War Diary	D.2.C.9.1 Sheet 36 A. N.E. 1/20.000.	28/08/1918	31/08/1918
Miscellaneous	Headquarter (A) 40th Division	02/10/1918	02/10/1918
War Diary	D.2.C.9.1 Ref Map. 36.a 1/40.000	01/09/1918	02/09/1918
War Diary	Petit Sec Bois	03/09/1918	10/09/1918
War Diary	Petit Sec Bois E.9.9.4.3	11/09/1918	16/09/1918
War Diary	Shyx House N Steenwerch R.16.d.9.2.	17/09/1918	20/09/1918
War Diary	Onxy House No Steentuerck A.16.d.9.2	21/09/1918	30/09/1918
Miscellaneous	Headquarters (A) 40th Division	02/11/1918	02/11/1918
War Diary	Onxy. House N. Steen Wereck A.16.d.8.2	01/10/1918	06/10/1918
War Diary	Weal House H. 1.6.7.9.	07/10/1918	17/10/1918
War Diary	Weal House H.1.6.9.9.	18/10/1918	18/10/1918
War Diary	N. Fort du Vert Galant D.29.b. 5.6	19/10/1918	21/10/1918
War Diary	Mouvaux F.2b.b.1.9	22/10/1918	26/10/1918
War Diary	Lannoy	27/10/1918	31/10/1918
Miscellaneous	Headquarter (A) 40th Division	03/12/1918	03/12/1918
War Diary	Lannoy	01/11/1918	31/12/1918
Miscellaneous	Headquarter (A) 40th Division	01/02/1919	01/02/1919
War Diary	Lannoy	01/01/1919	31/01/1919
Miscellaneous	A.G's The 40th Div	01/03/1919	01/03/1919
War Diary	Lannoy	01/02/1919	28/02/1919
Heading	D.P.C 3rd Echelon	02/04/1919	02/04/1919
War Diary	Lannoy	01/03/1919	28/03/1919
War Diary	Havre	29/03/1919	29/03/1919
War Diary	Conder City Camp Havre	30/03/1919	31/03/1919
War Diary	Cinder City Camp Le Havre	01/05/1919	31/05/1919
War Diary	Cuiden City Fiarrc	01/06/1919	11/06/1919
War Diary	No 21 Camp Harfleur	12/06/1919	31/07/1919
War Diary	Harfleur No 21 Camp	01/08/1919	31/08/1919
War Diary	No 21 Camp Harfleur	01/09/1919	08/10/1919
Miscellaneous	Stray /WO/95/M		

woods/peachy

40TH DIVISION

17TH BN WORCESTERSHIRE REGT
(PIONEERS)
MAY 1918 - ~~MAR 1919~~
1919 OCT

From UK

Army Form C. 2118.

WAR DIARY
or
INTELLIGENCE SUMMARY

(Erase heading not required.)

Instructions regarding War Diaries and Intelligence Summaries are contained in F. S. Regs., Part II. and the Staff Manual respectively. Title Pages will be prepared in manuscript.

War Diary
of
1st Line 1/5 Batt. 17th L. Batt. Nov 16
from Nov 1st 1916
to Nov 31st 1916

Place	Date	Hour	Summary of Events and Information	Remarks and references to Appendices

Unit: 14th Garrison Batt. Worcest Regt.

A.F.C. 2118.
War Diary.
Month of May.

Date	Diary	Syllabus of officer
1st.	The Battalion continued training at HAUTEVILLE in accordance with instructions received from G.O.C. 199 Bde AVESNES & COMTE. Memo. P. 966/4 of 29/4/18 (see Appendix I). P.F. work was continued for 5 hours a day in deepening revetting trenches by the two platoons not on training work. Platoons on training 4 hours a day. Special Courses continued Musketry or rifle range training in P.T. Signalling (16 men). Lewis Gun (16 men). 57 men reported sick.	FOW
2nd.	Training Special Courses & P.F. work as before. A conference of Battalion commanders was held at 8 de HQ. Instruction of Box respirators by Gas NCO. General instructions issued with regard to HAUTEVILLE sector. See Appendix II(a). 66 men reported sick.	FOW
3rd.	Training & P.F. work as before. Inspection of Box respirators by Bde Gas Officer. Lecture by Col. Thurston on Map reading to all officers & NCO's. Lecture by Batt Musketry officer to Platoon Commanders & NCO's on	

	Use of rifle, Lewis Gun, Machine Guns & Gas etc. 87 men reported sick.	FoW
4th	Training &c. work as before. Coy Commanders lectured to their Coys. on the General instructions with regard to the HAUTEVILLE Sector. 40 men reported sick.	FoW
5th	No PF work. a Training Church parade for Coff & RC. 58 men reported sick.	FoW
6th	All men on PF work. B&Staff took Platoon Commanders & 36 Senior NCOs in tactical exercise in the afternoon. Course of Musketry changed to 100 men put through rapid practice each day. 37 men reported sick.	FoW

7th.	R.E. work & Special training as before. 1st round of inter battalion Competition football played. B.d Staff took Platoon Commanders & 36 Senior NCO's in tactical exercise in the afternoon. 37 men reported sick.	30W
8th.	R.E. work & training as before. The Reserve Army Commander, General Sir H.P. Peyton, KCB. D.S.O. inspected the battalion at work. Batt orders as follows "The Army Commander expressed himself on detach from Batt orders as follows "The Army Commander expressed himself very well pleased with all he saw on this occasion. The C.O. desires his appreciation of the behaviour & all ranks."	30W
9th.	R.E. work & training as before. Special training as before. The following officers reported for duty. 2Lt. W.W. Ellis & Lt. Tuck & E. Hall & S. Smith	30W
10th.	R.E. work & training as before. Special training continued as before. B.d Signal Officers delivered a ball runner.	

		7ov

All ppies & parts of Capt. Hindes attended a lecture by
G.O.C. B'd at LATTRE St QUENTIN.
The undermentioned Officers reported for duty
after ed.
2/Lt - R.D. Carlisle. 6th P.P.C.L.I. Batt.
" A.P. Brown. 5th " " "
" L.H. Mansfield 2nd " " "
" V.E.D Dallas 4th " " "
" J. Riddell 4th " " "

2h men reported sick.

11th PE work training as before. Special course.   7ov
12th No PE work or training. Church parade. C.of E. + R.C.   7ov
       41 men reported sick.
13th PE work training as before.
       Platoon commanders & NCO's were instructed in reconnoitring &
       fighting patrols by the Musketry instructor. 36 men reported sick.   7ov

14th	P.F. work & special training as before. Lecture in afternoon. Section Fire Control. Battalion manned Battle Stations from 9 to 9.30 pm. the whole practice being carried out in gas masks. 33 men reported sick. FTW
15th.	P.F. work & Special training as before. Lecture on inspection of messages by the afternoon to platoon Commanders & NCO's. 47 men reported sick. FTW
16th	P.F. work & special training as before. Tactical Scheme for platoon commanders & NCO's in the afternoon. 44 men reported sick. FTW.
17th	P.F. work & special training as before. Afternoon lecture in map reading. 31 men reported sick. FTW
18th	P.F. work & training as before. Afternoon football match. Officers v Cooks evening FTW

		Four

evening.
Battalion concert party gave their first concert
in hut next to Batt. Canteen.

19th. Instructions received by telephone from G.O.C. 176 Bde at 12.50
p.m. for the Battalion to move, during the afternoon to
HABARCQ
The Battalion moved at 5.45 p.m.
Transport & Lewis Gun Limbers & G.S. Waggons (incl. C.T. Mellis
Cart). Information was received that 2 G.S. Lorries would
be sent the following morning to Hauteville. Ammunition
(88 boxes - S.A.A. - Rifle) however was crowded, that a report
was to be sent of the number of Lorries required to turn.
the views back. The surplus Stores & Kits direct to Division.
(5 Lorries were added fr.) 1 rear party was left at HAUTEVILLE.
2/40 men (under 2nd Lt. Tubraj) + 2 Guards. 2/Lt. Hutchinson & 2/Lt. Mansfield
with instructions to guard Stores, Batt. Ammunition reserve & to
clean up billets and camping grounds - Certificate to this effect

	FOW
	was obtained by Sgt Hixson from the Area Commandant. Sgt Hixson handed over all his secret documents relative to the defence of the HAUTEVILLE Sector, to the Area Commandant FOSSEUX 26 men reported sick
20th	The Battalion moved from HBARCQ at 6 am (Normal Order see Appendix II) The R.C. No. 1 Sec. was present when the Battalion moved from the starting point to the village. Notification was received (guns not 10 lorries would report at 9 am to take men unable to march. The march from HAUTEVILLE to HATORICQ was 9 kilometres - had heavy rain each one 70 men were unable to march. It was considered that, none of the chief duties of the Battalion was to form a correct estimate of the capability of the men to undergo physical strain, it was not advisable to leave men behind - the could encourage the men by fallout - A reasonably large % of a NCO + 12 men under the Batt Sergt + Sgt Brown to clean rifles. load blank ammunition on the lorries + guide them to the destination with instructions to pick

up any men on the road who had been unable to proceed. A midday halt was made near VILLERS BRULIN, at 8 a.m. The march was resumed at 4 p.m. Arrival at HOUVELIN Thm. Billets allotted to the Battalion were found to be in occupation of 5th Provisional Garrison Guard Batt. 126 men fell out during the last mile. The great heat was partially the cause of this.

21st The Battalion continued the march (mentioned order see appendix II) 240 men were unable to march. 10 lorries were sent to Bn from the (estimator (FIEFS) These lorries were sent back to BAILLEUL with 5 the midday halt was made. I brought the remainder of the men to the destination in successive journeys. The great heat of the day was sources chiefly the cause of the exhausted condition of the men. From the experience of these two days march the Medical Officer considered that the great majority of the men would be unable to march for more than 2 consecutive days, + for not more than 8 miles a day.

22nd	A report was made by the Medical Officer that a large proportion of the men would be unable to continue the march.	7 T.N.
22nd	Orders were received that there would be no move. Inspection of billets at 10 a.m. Medical inspection of the whole Battalion by the Medical Officer	7 T.N.
23rd	Orders received that there would be no move. Inspection of billets 10 a.m. Open air concert 6 p.m.	7 T.N.
24th	The Battalion continued the march. (movement orders see Appendix I) Destination BLESSY. (distance 11 miles approx) weather, cool, heavy rain beforehand. A halt of 2 hours was made near COHEM. 240 men were left behind & were brought up by lorries 270 N.S.	7 T.N.
25th	The march was resumed. Destination No 3 Camp CLARQUES. (movement orders Appendix II) Designation of Battalion changed. (7 Worcestershire to 17th Garrison Batt. Worcestershire Regt. Report by M.O. on physical incapabilities of Bin. Appendix III.	

26th	Sunday. The Battalion paraded at 2.30 & training was continued until 1.15. as notification had been received from Bde that an officer from I.H.Q. would inspect the battalion while turned out. The 90 C. Bde was present. The inspecting officer did not come. The following officers visited Lieut. N.C. Wood, Lieut. S.W. Foster, 2/Lt. I.C. Sunderson, 2/Lt. Jeffry, 2/Lt. Hey, 2/Lt. R. Holtzapfel, 2/Lt. J. Doyle, 2/Lt. C.J.P. Vandestelen, 2/Lt. R.J. Luck, 2/Lt. Squires. FON
27th	Inspection of L & g Field Coys R.E. S.574. 41.25.5.15 in accordance with 176 Bde instructions (see Appendix 1) Kit inspection at 3 p.m. Number officers on R.E. work taken on special courses (Appendix III Parade States). L5 men reported sick. FON
28th	R.E. work as before. 1 hours training. The following officers rejoined their battalion in accordance with instructions received from 176 Bde.

28th		
29th	2/Lt. / Mr. Mansfield	FW
	" / 2nd. Dallas.	
	" Riddell	FW
	DR Carlisle	
	95 men reported sick	
29th	OF wrote & turning a-begns	FW
	Batt. Standing oder isined Appendix II a.	
	78 men reported sick	
30th	RF wrote & forming as before.	FW
	74 men reported sick	
31st	RF wrote & turning a-before.	FW
	44 men reported sick.	

1/5/17. Isaac Wtt
Lt. 4th Garrison Bn
att. 7th Lincolnshire Regt.

Appendix
I

Bde instructions
Ref? training
& Rft. work.

Training Programme
for W.E. 4-5-1918. See
199 Brigade Gishchi
dated 29/4/18.
Copy with 199 Brigade
War Diary

T/6.

Appendix I.

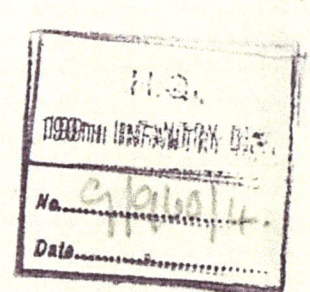

Northern Sector,
Southern Sector,
1st Provisional G.G.Bn.
2nd   "   "   "
3rd   "   "   "
4th   "   "   "
5th   "   "   "
4th Garr. Bn. Royal Welsh Fus.
War Diary - 2 copies.

    Herewith Training Programme for week ending 4.5.18.

    Whenever possible, care must be taken that no damage is done to crops during the training.

                                               Captain,
                                        Brigade Major,
27.4.18.   199th Infantry Brigade.

Appendix "H"

Movement Orders No 1 & 2

Other more instructions contained in

176 Infantry Brigade Order No 109 May 18th & accompanying
March Table "A"

Memorandum No 1 to 176 Bde Order No 109

176 Infantry Brigade March Table "B" - May 19th
176 Infantry Brigade March Table "C"
176 Brigade Addendum No 1 to March "C", "19th"

SECRET.   Copy No. 2

1st Provisional Garrison Guard Battalion.

OPERATION ORDER No.2.

20th MAY 1918.

1. MOVE.	The Battalion will move on the 21st inst.
2. STARTING POINT.	Fork roads at O.22.b.3.3.
3. ROUTE.	BAJUS – LE THIEULOYE – VALHUON – TANGRY – SAINS Les PERNS – FIEFS.
4. ORDER OF MARCH.	The Battalion will march in the following order and will pass the starting point at 5-10 a.m. :- Headquarters Staff. No.2 Company. No.3 Company. No.4 Company. No.1 Company. Police. Rear guard. (1 platoon No.1 Company, O.C. Capt. Cradock.
5. HALT.	Will be notified later. The march will be resumed at 4-0 p.m.
6. DESTINATION.	2nd day. FIEFS.
7. REPORTS.	To head of column (No.2 Company).
8. DETAIL.	Battalion Orders of the 20th Inst.
9. REAR GUARD.	4 N.C.Os. from No.1 Company will be detailed by Capt. Cradock.

Major & Adjutant.
1st Provisional Garrison Guard Battn.

DISTRIBUTION.
Copy No.1, O.C. No.1 Company.
" No.2, O.C. No.2 Company.
" No.3, O.C. No.3 Company.
" No.4, O.C. No.4 Company.
" No.5, Quartermaster.
" No.6, Transport Officer.
" No.7, Medical Officer.
" No.8, Billeting Officer.
" No.9, R.S.M.
" No.10, File.

Appendix II.
(a).

1. General instructions with regard to the defence of the HAUTEVILLE Sector.
2. Standing orders at rest & on the march.

17th Garr. Battn. Worcestershire Regiment.

STANDING ORDERS WHEN ON THE MARCH.

1. MARCH DISCIPLINE. Intervals of 150 yards between Companies and 500 yards between Battalions will be maintained on the march, and special attention will be paid to march discipline.

2. DEFENCE. Companies will detail one section each for defence against aircraft, whose duties will be in accordance with instructions issued to Company Commanders.
These sections will march in rear of their Companies and will be commanded by an Officer.

3. TRANSPORT. Special motor transport will be provided for ammunition, blankets and packs.
Blankets will be rolled in bundles of 10 and marked by Companies.

4. MEN'S KIT. The following will be the distribution of men's kit :-

On the man.	On Transport.
Equipment & rifle, with 120 rds. S.A.A.	Pack, containing Greatcoat,
Ground sheet.	Housewife,
Steel helmet.	One pair socks,
Hold-all.	Cap comforter,
One pair socks.	Entrenching tool.
Iron rations.	
Towel and soap.	NOTE. Entrenching tool will be
Cleaning kit.	carried on the Transport
Box Respirator.	only if not proceeding for
Mess Tin.	active operations.

Company Commanders are responsible that the contents of packs are as detailed above.
Ammunition, packs and blankets will be dumped in charge of the guard at a place to be assigned in Battalion Orders, and fatigue parties will be detailed by Companies for this purpose.

5. LIMBERS. One limber will accompany each Company, and will be loaded with rations, dixies, petrol tins filled with drinking water, and mess stores.
The time of loading will be under Company arrangements.
Limbers will report to the Transport Officer when Companies move to the starting point.
Limbers will report to Companies on arrival at destination.
No Officers' kits are to be loaded on them.

6. G.S. WAGONS. The place where G.S. wagons will be loaded will be given in Battalion Orders.
A loading party will invariably be detailed as follows :-
2 men from each Company and 1 N.C.O. from Company on duty.
This party will report to the Transport Officer one hour before the time given in Battalion orders for G.S. wagons to be loaded.

7. BILLETS. The Billeting Officer and his party will invariably report to the Town Major, Area Commandant or representative at the destination before 9-0 a.m. of the day on which the march takes place.
The Billeting Officer's party will be composed of :-
Company Quartermaster Sergeants.
1 N.C.O. and 1 man per Company to act as guides.
The Billeting Officer is responsible for arranging with Company Commanders the time and place of parade of this

7. **BILLETS** (contd).
party, and for making all arrangements for the move, and for rations if necessary.
He will assign places for the guides to meet the Battalion and conduct to Billets.
He will apply to the Adjutant for information with reference to destination.
Pioneers and sanitary squad will accompany this party.

The Pioneer Sergeant will be responsible that latrines are constructed before the arrival of the Battalion at destination. He will report to the Billeting Officer for information with regard to the position of billets or camping grounds.
He will apply to the Area Commandant for tools, etc.

8. **REAR PARTY.**
A rear party will invariably be detailed when on the march, and will be composed as follows :-
    1 N.C.O. and 4 men from each Company for cleaning Company billets.
    2 men from each Company and 1 N.C.O. from Company on duty for cleaning Headquarter billets.
The Company for duty will detail the Officer to command, who will obtain the necessary certificate from the Billet Warden, and will arrange with Company Commanders for time and place of parade of this party, and for rations if necessary.
The certificate will invariably be rendered to Battalion Orderly Room signed by the Billet Warden to the effect that the billets vacated by the Battalion have been left in a clean and sanitary condition.

T.W.T. Deane Lt Col
OC 7th G'rn Worcestershire Regt

STANDING ORDERS WHEN AT REST.

1. **GUARD. DUTIES OF COMMANDER.**

   a. The Commander of the Guard will be responsible that when taking over he thoroughly understands the duties of his particular guard, and of his sentries, and that everything in and around the guard is in perfect order before finally taking over from the old guard.

   b. He will see that the sentries perform their duties, and that they move about on their posts in a proper manner.

   c. He will frequently visit his sentries both by day and night to see that they are alert on their posts.

   d. He will see that his sentries pay proper compliments, and instruct them as to their procedure when it becomes necessary for the guard to be turned out.

   e. He will turn out the guard at Reveille, Retreat and Tattoo, and at these times will thoroughly inspect his guard before dismissing them.
   He will turn out his guard to all armed parties, and to all General Officers. He will turn out his guard, when Battalion guard, once by day to the Commanding Officer.

   f. He will obtain a copy of charge against any man confined in his guard room from the person placing him in custody.

   g. He is responsible that the men of his guard, and all prisoners under his charge are cleaned up, washed and shaved before 8-0 a.m.

   h. If an alarm is given he will immediately inform the Adjutant and Regimental Sergeant Major, and stand to arms until dismissed by an Officer.

   j. He will at once report any unusual occurrence which takes place within his vision.

   k. He will see that his guard and prisoners get their meals at the proper hours.

   l. He will allow no N.C.O. or man of his guard to take off their clothing or accoutrements during his tour of duty except during morning wash and brush up, and then only two men at a time.

   m. He will be responsible for the safe custody of all prisoners in detention.

2. **BATTALION GUARD - DUTIES OF SENTRY.**

   a. To prevent any unauthorised person from taking anything left in charge of the guard without informing the guard commander.

   b. To prevent anyone taking water from the water cart for washing purposes.

   c. In case of fire to inform the commander of the guard immediately.

   d. He will challenge all persons entering or leaving camp between Tattoo and Reveille, and detain anyone who cannot satisfactorily explain his presence

3. **PROVOST SERGEANT.**

   The Provost Sergeant will superintend the unloading of special transport carrying blankets, packs and ammunition, and ensure that the ammunition is taken over by the guard at once, and that packs and blankets are correctly distributed to Companies.
   He will report to the R.S.M. for instructions with regard to bounds and duties and positions of police to meet the requirements imposed by the circumstances under which the Battalion is placed at the time.

3. **SANITARY.** The Sanitary Corporal will parade Sanitary men quarter of an hour after reveille each day. He will then assign them their duties up to the breakfast hour, which will be cleaning up the ground upon which night urine tubs have been placed, and the carrying out of special instructions issued by the Medical Officer.
He will see that the urine tubs are emptied in the place allotted for this purpose.
The emptying of night urine tubs will be performed under Company arrangements between reveille and the time at which the sanitary men parade.
The Sanitary Corporal will parade the sanitary men and light duty men at 9 o'clock daily in front of the Medical Inspection room.
He will take note of the duties which have to be performed during the day from the Medical Officer, and see that these are carried out.
He will allot to the light duty men the area of the camp which they have to clean, and will not dismiss them until the camp is thoroughly sanitary.
He will see that the ablution places are in proper order by 10-0 a.m. daily, and that no washing is carried on in other places than those allotted.
He will be responsible that the incinerator is working properly.
He will be responsible that all dirty water is emptied into the place allotted, and that there is no fouling of any ground.
He will be responsible that grease traps are provided near all cookhouses.
He will be entirely responsible for the cleanliness and general tidiness of the camp outside all Company areas, where he must not interfere but merely advise, reporting to the Medical Officer any contravention of the standing Sanitary orders in connection with the Company areas.

4. **SERGEANT COOK.** The Sergeant Cook is entirely responsible to the Quartermaster for the cooking of the food of the Battalion.
He will see that the food for cooking is put on the fire in sufficient time to be served at the times defined in orders, or according to instructions received from Companies.
He will make himself acquainted with Company orders each evening with the object of ascertaining whether any meals have to be served at times other than those stated in Battalion Orders.
He will see that there is no shortage of fuel, exercising sufficient control over its use to maintain, if possible a reserve.
He will see that food never comes in contact with the earth, and that boxes or wood on which meat is cut up are scrubbed with boiling water and soap after use daily.
He will see that cooks are clean in their person, washed and shaved at all times, and that particular attention is paid to their hands and nails, which must be clean.
He will be responsible to the Quartermaster that the number of cooks is maintained.
He will arrange with Companies to have supernumaries under training as cooks as far as it is practicable.
He will see that Companies keep a stock pot so that hot soup may be available for men at night.

5.	DAMAGE to TREES, CROPS, etc.	It is strictly forbidden to cause damage to trees, hedges, or fences, or to walk or ride through growing crops. All ranks must proceed along the edge of cultivated ground, and so prevent damage being caused, and claims made by civilians.
6.	DRESS.	No man is allowed to leave camp or billet unless properly dressed, i.e. with belt and puttees. Whether Box Respirators are to be carried will be published in Battalion Orders.
7.	LIGHTS.	No lights are to be shown in the camp after dark (9-0 p.m. June and July).
8.	ROUTINE.	All ranks will be in camp at 9-30 p.m. Staff parade and Lights Out, 10-0 p.m.
9.	TENTS.	Tents will be struck and removed from their ground every second day.
10.	BLANKETS.	Blankets will be hung out each day for several hours. Lines will be stretched in rear of the tents for this purpose and the general tidiness of the camp will be observed in the arrangement of lines.
11.	BARBERS.	Barbers will keep a careful record in A.B.136 of the number of men whose hair they cut, and report to Battalion Orderly Room with this book at 2-0 p.m. each Saturday. Barbers shop will be open from 3-0 p.m. to 6-0 p.m. each day.
12.	PERSONNEL PROCEEDING ON COURSES etc.	The Battalion Orderly Sergeant will be responsible that all parties of men leaving the Battalion on special duty or on leave parade at the time appointed, and that the N.C.O. in charge is in possession of written instructions from the Adjutant. All parties will parade at Battalion Orderly Room and be inspected by the Orderly Officer before leaving.

TW. Isaac Lt Col
O.C. 17th Gar. Bn.
Worcestershire Regt

ORDERS FOR THE PREVENTION OF FIRES.

1. Striking of matches, kindling of fires, smoking, and the use of naked lights even in candlesticks, in or near buildings containing straw, hay, or similar inflammable material, are strictly forbidden. No candle will be lighted in any building or room unless it is stuck in a lantern or improvised candlestick.

2. No lighted brazier is to be inside any building where there is straw, hay, or other inflammable material.

3. The indiscriminate erection or use of extemporised fireplaces in or near barns or other buildings occupied by troops is prohibited.

4. No stove or fireplace will be erected in any billet unless it has been inspected by a R.E. Officer, who will be responsible that it is safely constructed.

5. When stoves are fixed in huts or other buildings, care is to be taken that no part of the metal flue touches any woodwork.

6. All stoves should stand upon a non-inflammable platform.

7. Some protection should be placed round stoves having open doors or any aperture from which hot cinders can fall on the floor.

8. Flues must be regularly swept.

9. A daily inspection of all woodwork near stoves and flues should be made to ascertain that there is no charring of wood in progress.

10. Fires should be extinguished at "Lights Out", and the ashes removed outside the building.

11. Special care will be paid to the strict observance of "Lights Out"; fires will be put out and not "banked" at "Lights Out" or earlier.

12. The storage of bombs, explosives, or ammunition in billets occupied by troops is forbidden.

13. A tin of dry earth or sand and a tin of water will be kept in in each billet, ready to throw on any fire immediately it breaks out.

14. No lighted candle or brazier is to be left burning in a billet unless some person remains present in the billet.

15. All billets in which troops are quartered will be frequently visited at uncertain hours to see that these instructions are carried out.

T.W. Leane Lt Col
OC 17th G. Bn
Worcestershire Regt

CONFIDENTIAL.

NOTES ON GUARD MOUNTING.

The Battalion Orderly Sergeant will report to the Orderly Officer when the guard is paraded and ready for inspection at the appointed place.

The orders given by the B.O.S. will be as follows :—

1. Guard – "Attention".

2. Fix Bayonets.

   (If in two ranks, "rear rank, one pace step back, march").

3. Guard – Right dress.
   The N.C.O. i/c. guard aligns himself with the front rank and dresses it.
   (If in two ranks the senior Orderly Sergeant will dress the rear rank).

   The Orderly Officer will then inspect the guard as regards equipment, cleanliness, and general turnout.

4. Guard – "unfix, bayonets".

5. "For inspection port arms".
   Rifles will then be inspected.
   After the inspection (if in two ranks "Guard, attention. Close ranks, march").

6. Guard. "fix, bayonets".

7. Slope arms.

8. To your post –
   (On this command the N.C.O. i/c guard will at once take post in rear of the guard)
   Quick march.

Officers should note carefully the following points:—

(a) Always to leave an interval between commands. One movement must be correctly completed and a short interval left before the next command is given.

(b) Give the cautionary word slowly, and the executive word of command quickly, distinctly and sharply. It is most difficult for men to move smartly and together if there is any length of sound in the word of command — some will move at the beginning of the sound and some at the end.

Appendix II to War Diary
(b)

Parade States.
from 28th to 31st May

Battalion Employ

Duties	1	2	3	4		1	2	3	4	HQ
Work in Trenches	156	146	142	149	R.S.M.					
Musketry Course		1			R.Q.M.S.					1
Brigade Guard					Orderly Room Staff		2	1		3
Battalion Guard	4	4	5		Military Police					1
" Employ	20	18	17	16	M.O's Orderlies	2		1	2	2
Company Employ	15	14	25	23	Cooks (H.Q. O.M.)	2	1			1
Sick	4	4	5		Pioneers	1				1
Hospital	7	4	10	10	Shoemakers	2	1	4	2	2
Signalling Course	7	6	3	1	Tailors	2			3	2
Refugees					Officers' Servants	1	1	1	1	
Company Parade Ings					Armis Mess Staff					
Detention				1	Brigade Pioneers	2	2			
Other Courses	7	8	11	7	Battalion Runners					1
On Command	7	5		3	Q.M. Storemen	1			1	
Leave			3		Runners	1				
Absent		1			Orderlies	1				
					Clerks	1	1			
					Post Corporal				1	
					Company Duties	2	3	2	3	
					Canteen	1	1			
					Signallers (Ord. Rm)		2	2		
					Gas N.C.O.					
					Transport	5	2	5	4	
					R.S.M. Servant		1			
					C.O. Groom					

Company Employ

	1	2	3	4
Cooks	4	4	4	4
C.Q.M.S.	1	1	1	1
Company Storemen	1	1	1	1
Clerk	1	1	1	1
Pioneer		1	1	1
Co. Ord. Sergt.	1	1	1	1
Staff	1	1	1	1
Officers' Cooks		1		
Servants	5	5	4	5
Batt. Ord. Sergt. Corpl.	1		1	
M.O. Fatigues (Pickets)	1		1	6
Billet Watchers	4			2
Wood Fatigue				
Loss of Fatigues				

May 31st 1918.

Duties	1	2	3	4		Battalion Employ	1	2	3	4	HQ		Company Employ	1	2	3	4
Week in Trenches	156	148	152	155		R.S.M.					1		Cooks	4	4	4	4
Working Parties		1				R.Q.M.S.					1						
Ration Parties						Orderly Room Staff					3		C.Q.M.S.	1	1	1	1
Battalion Duties						M.chy Police	2	1	1	1			Company Storeman	1	1	1	1
Battalion Employ	5	5				M.O. Orderlies					2						
Company Employ	20	18	17	16		Cooks (HQ.O.R.s)	2	1	1		1		Clerk	1	1	1	1
Company Employ	15	16	22	20		Pioneers	2	1	4	2	2		Pioneer	1	1	1	1
Sick	3	8	3	15		Shoemakers	1	1	1	3	2		Co. Orderly	1	1	1	1
Hospital	7	4	10	10		Tailors				1			Lewis Gun	1		1	1
Signalling Course	7	6		1		Officers Servants	1	1	1	1							
Fatigues						Officers Mess Staff	2	1	1				Officers' Cook				1
Company Grenade Inst						Brigade Runners	1		2				Servants	5	5	4	5
Attention			1			Battalion Runners		2					Fatigue Cart Staff	1			
Officer Course	7	8	14	7		Q.M. Storemen	1						Cook	1			
On Command	3	3				Gypsies	1	1		1							
Leave			3	1		Butchers	1	1					M.O. Fatigue (orderlies)	2	3	2	3	5
Absent		1				Clerk				1			Orderly Room	1			3
						Post Corporal	2	2					Officer Orderlies		2	2		
						Company Buglers	1			1			Mess Fatigue	1			
						Sanitation (O.R. Rm)	5	2	5	4			Troop Fatigue	4			
						Signal N.C.O.	1										
						Stretcher											
						R.S.M. Servant											

May 30th 1918

Duties	1	2	3	4	Battalion Employ	1	2	3	4	HQ	Company Employ	1	2	3	4
Work in Trenches	144	148	152	139	R.S.M.					1	Cooks	4	4	4	4
					R.Q.M.S.					1					
Musketry Course		1			Orderly Room Staff		2			3	C.Q.M.S.	1	1	1	1
Brigade Guard					Military Police	2		1			Company Storemen	1	1	1	1
Battalion Guard	5			5	A.O.'s Orderlies		1			2	" Clerk	1	1	1	1
Battalion Employ	20	18	17	16	Cooks (H.Q, Q.M etc)	2	1	4	2	1	" Runner	1			
Company Employ	22	15	23	17	" Pioneers	2				2	Com. Ord. Sergt	1	1	1	1
Sick	10	13	4	22	Shoemakers	1	1		1						
Hospital	7	4	9	7	Tailors	1	1	1	3		" Sergt	1			1
Signalling Course		6		1	Officers Servants		1				Officers Cooks	1	1	1	1
Religion					Officers Mess Staff	2	2				" Servants	5	5	4	7
Company Cadre Inf.					Brigade Runners	1					Batt. Ord. Sergt.	1	1		
Rifleshove				1	Battalion Runners	1			1		" Sergt.	1			
Other Courses		9	13	10	Q.M. Storemen	1		1		1	M.O. Stretcherbearer		1	4	
					Grocer	2	3	2	3	1	Rolls Orderlies	5	1	4	
Command		1			Butchers	1	1				Wood fatigue				
Leave			3	1	Clerk	2	2	2			Camp				
Absent		1			Post Corporal				1						
					Sanitary Duties	5	2	5	4						
					Lawlers			1							
					Lagrallier (at. Bn.)		1								
					Yen N.C.O										
					Bandsmen										
					R.S.M Servant										
					C.O's Groom										

20th May 1918.

Duties					Battalion Employ					Company Employ				
	1	2	3	4		1	2	3	4		1	2	3	4
Strength	152	150	144											
Instrs. Personnel		1			R.S.M.					Cooks	4	4	4	4
					R.Q.M.S.									
Details				5	Orderly Room Staff					C.Q.M.S.	1	1	1	1
Orderly Room					Sergt. Pioneers	2	1	1	1					
Sick (H.Q. & H.S.)	22	20	16	15	A.C. Cyclists		1		2	Company Storemen	1	1	1	1
Leave	21	12	23	23	Ch. Kr. (H.Q. Coy.)	2	1	4	1	Batmen	1	1	1	1
Company Employ	7	8	6	12	Leave	2	1		1	Pioneers	1	1	1	1
Sick	8	4	7	4	Shoemakers	1	1	1	2	Sec. Sect. Sgt.	1	1	1	1
					Tailors	1	1	1	2	Snipers				
Employment	3	6		1	Officers Servants	2		3		Assist Sergts.	1	1	1	1
Imprisonment					Pioneers	1	1	1		Officer's Cooks	1		1	
	3				Mess Orderly Staff	2		1						
					Assist. Signallers					Pioneers		1	1	8
Employment Persml. Sig.					Waterers	1								
Pilots				1	Orderlies	1	1		1	Batt. Ord. Staff	6	5	4	1
					Armrs.					Bugler				
		8	13	10	Post Corporal	2	3	2	3	N.C.O.(Signallers)	1	1		1
					Orderly Sheet					Pulls Cleaners	5	4	4	3
Personnel	1				Bondism					N.C.O. & Signaller				
					(signallers Batmn)									
Leave		3	1		Ser. M.O.	1	2	2	1	Leave				
Deaths					Bandsmen									
Notes	17°	1			R.S.M. Servant	5	4	3	3					
Imprisonment etc.				5	A.C.O. Signs		1							
		28 May 1918												

War Diary –
Appendix IV.
Medical. PW

MEDICAL.

The Battalion was formed on the 15th April at ETAPLES of men of various medical categories, B1 and lower.

It was obvious that the medical side of its administration was to receive special attention in order

- (a) to test to what extent these men could be used in marching and in active operations in or near the front line.
- (b) To supply reliable information with regard to this in order that personnel of these categories might be most usefully employed in future.

The Medical Officer's report of the conclusions arrived at since he joined the Battalion on 23/4/1918 is as follows:-

"The Battalion is composed of very varied elements. Some
"of the men are Category B1, others have been boarded as
"permanently unfit or for permanent base duty only.
"25 suffer from organic disease of the heart. A much
"larger number suffer from irregularity of the heart action
"(D.A.H.) which lessens working efficiency.
"40 suffer from rupture and 65 from the effects of old
"wounds. Approximately 100 can be put under the heading
"'Debility'. This debility is due to such causes as -
"Poor physique, Defective feet, Age, Asthma & Bronchitis,
"Chronic Rheumatism and old Tubercular trouble.
"As regards marching approximately 70 are unable to march
"8 miles per day without packs. 100 are unfit for duty
"in the line owing to other physical disabilities.
"On the march to the present camp the men marched in
"'Fighting Order' without packs.
"My opinion is that the great majority of the men
"are unfit to march more than 8 miles per day for more
"than two days together, and over 100 are unfit to do even
"that and be of any value for some time after.
"As regards the work at present the men are very unequally
"qualified for it - some men who have been made B1 for
"ear troubles or sight are perfectly fit for the walking
"and digging. To others, with heart conditions, the work is
"a danger.
" A certain number of the men are benefitting by their
"training, but for others with poor physique and heart
"troubles life here is proving too severe and is wearing
"them down.
"The Battalion is to be allowed to send away this week
"a certain number of the worst cases. This number is
"indefinite at present.
"My opinion is that a complete rest on Sundays would not
"result in less work being done in the long run. This
"has proved itself true in munition factories.
"I strongly recommend that the task work be given in
"groups so that the strong may help the weak.
" The tasks should be varied according to the character
"of the soil. I understand that the latter is done in
"theory but not in practice.

"As regards holding the line, 20% to 30% are fit in a quiet
"sector in the summer months. A number of men with heart
"trouble would suffer under shell fire and probably be useless
"A number of men who have suffered from shell shock would
"probably be in the same condition.

"The usual marching, incidental to holding the line,
"would be beyond the capacity of most of the men.
"On the occasion of another march, travelling kitchens
"and two proper water carts would be of great value.
"If the hundred worst marchers are eliminated, in my
"opinion, on another march a Motor Ambulance would be
sufficient to deal with the stragglers, if the march is
"8 miles a day for 2 days followed by a day's rest."

This report is of the state of the Battalion on the 6th June.

Men had been evacuated as follows :-

    27 to No.283 Area Employment Co.   26/5/18.
    13 to No.284   "   "   "   "
    44 to Casualty Clearing Stations, between 23/4/18 and
                                                    2/6/18.

GARRISON GUARD BRIGADE G.960/4.
TRAINING PROGRAMME
29.4.18-4.5.18.

1. ### 1st DAY.

Two platoons per Company will be on work. The remaining Platoons will train as follows :-

'A' Platoon will man its own front line trenches.
'B' Platoon will carry out attack from distance of 1000 yards.
'A' Platoon will make note of mistakes made by 'B' Platoon and a short conference will be held on completion of exercise.
These platoons will then change places and the same procedure will be adopted.
The third practice will be carried out when the Company H.Q's Staff critisise.

NOTE - These exercises must not be rushed, and if the third cannot be carried out in the morning it will be carried out on the third day of training.

2nd DAY.

As for 1st Day but with the other two platoons per Company.

3rd DAY.

See 1st Day, remainder of time to be spent as follows :-

    1 hour - ~~~~~~~~~~.
    1 " - Coy. drill.
Remainder of morning, musketry.
Afternoon - Battalion parade for half-an-hour.

4th DAY.

As for 3rd Day, but with the other 2 platoons per Company.

5th DAY.

Half Battalion attack their own trenches from 4000 yards in front.

6th DAY.

As for 5th Day, but with other half Battalion.

2. The B.G.C. will meet all Battalion Officers at Battalion Orderly Room at 2.30 p.m. as follows :-

4th Garr.Bn. Royal Welsh Fus.	29th inst.
1st Provisional G.G.Bn.	30th "
2nd " " "	1st May.
3rd " " "	2nd "
4th " " "	3rd "
5th " " "	4th "

He will then conduct a tactical exercise in the neighbourhood of their own trenches. Each Officer in possession of a map will bring it, also pencil and note book

Continued......

(2).

3. (a) Battalions will arrange one lectures during the week.
   (b) Sector Commanders will arrange one lecture during the week.
   (c) The Brigade Staff will give one lecture during the week to each Battalion, and Battalions will inform Brigade H.Q. as soon as possible on which of the following subjects they would like a lecture given :-

   1. Lessons learnt during recent operations.
   2. History and siting of trenches.
   3. Use of Rifle, Lewis Gun and Machine Gun.
   4. Writing of orders and messages.
   5. Ration supply in the field.

4. Day manning of trenches will be discontinued during this period, but trenches will be manned from 9 - 9.30 p.m. on May 1st.1918, the whole practice being carried out in gas masks.

5. Musketry for particularly backward men.

6. Gas Drill. Orders to put on gas masks should be given at intervals and unexpected moments during the training.

27.4.18.

Each Battalion party of 600 will be divided into 4 parties of 150 each.

4. (b) R.E. guides from 46th Field Co. R.E. will report at 6.30 a.m. 27th May, at Battalion Headquarters of the 1st & 2nd Iron. G.G. Battns. Parties will be told off as in para (a) above.

5. Tools for units of BILQUES sub-sector will be delivered to their Headquarters on 26th instant.

Units of REBECQ sub-sector will arrange to draw tools from Headquarters, 46th Field Co. R.E. CLARQUES, tomorrow, the 26th inst.

6. The task allotted is 8 linear feet of trench per man to a depth of 1'9" first day, the trench being dug to a depth of 3'6" the second day
(See attached diagram)

It is of the utmost importance that the task should be completed. The task allotted is small in order that there may be no doubt about its completion to time.

7. The utmost care is to be taken to avoid unnecessary damage to crops. Troops will not be allowed to make short cuts across fields, but will be taken along the line of trench when necessary.

Sd. R. Taylor.
Captain, Brigade Major
1/6th Infantry Brigade

25.5.18

Copy/Secret   S.46   S.7/1
                                                    25.5.18

1st Pror. G.G. Bn.
4th   "   "
5th   "   "
4th Garr. Battn. R.W. Fus.
C.R.E. D Sector.
469th Field Co. R.E.
431st Field Co. R.E.

1. The 176th Infantry Brigade will commence to dig "D" sector
   "B.B" Line on Monday, 27th May from Southern Boundary -
   G.33.d.2.7 to Northern boundary - F.11.d.8.2.

2. The sector is divided into two sub-sectors as follows:-
        REBECQ sub-sector.   SOUTHERN
        BILQUES   "   "   NORTHERN
   Dividing line between sub-sectors is the stream in L.11.6.
   The 1st & 5th Pror. G.G. Battalions will be responsible for
   the Southern Sector.
   The 4th Pror. G.G. Battn. & 4th Garrison Battn. R.W. Fus
   will be responsible for the Northern sector.

3. Each Battalion will furnish daily 100 (Other ranks)
   for digging.

4. (a) On Monday, 27th May R.E. guides from 431st Field Co
   will report at 4th Pror. G.G. Battn. & 4th Garr. Battn. R.W Fus.
   Headquarters at the rate of 4 per Battalion at
   6.30am

(W5)

17th Gn. Bn. Norf. Regt.
23rd Gn. Bn. Lanc. Fus.
17th Gn. Bn. Royal Sussex R.
4th Gn. Bn. R. Welsh Fus.

1. The G.O.C. Brigade wishes that Units should take rifles & fighting order when proceeding to dig.
Rifles & equipment should be laid out "behind" each man's task clear of the earth excavated.
Alarms should be practised once or twice while men are at work on their tasks.

2. On arrival at work each platoon must have a latrine dug, which must be filled in on completion of the day's task.

3. Re. Walking out dress — Gas helmets need not be carried in this area as it is not in the Precautionary Zone.

(Signed) R. Grant L.
for Captain Brigade Major
16th Infantry Brigade

27.5.16

SECRET. Copy No.

1st Provisional Garrison Guard Battalion.

OPERATION ORDER No. 1.

19th MAY 1918.

Reference Sheet 51,c. 1/40,000.

1. INTENTION.	The 176 Brigade is moving North for work on a sector between AIRE and ST. OMER.
	The Battalion will move on the 20th inst. and will pass the starting point at 5-20 a.m.
STARTING POINT.	Cross K.8.c.9.0.6.5. in the village of HABARCQ *Italian gate* ~~Fork roads opposite Quartermaster's Stores, J.34.d.95.95.~~
3. ROUTE.	HERMAVILLE- Fork Roads - D.10a.4.2 -VILLERS-BRULIN ~~AVESNES - MANIN - PENIN - TINQUES - CHELERS - HOUVELIN~~ FREVILLERS.
4. ORDER OF MARCH.	Battalions will march in the following order, and will pass the starting point at the times stated, :-
	5th North Staffs. Training Cadre, 5-15 a.m.
	1st Prov. Garrison Guard Battn. 5-20 a.m. *5 a.m.*
	5th Prov. Garrison Guard Battn. 5-32 a.m.
	Order of march of 1st Prov. Garr. Guard Battn :-
	Headquarters Staff.
	No.4 Company.
	No.3 Company.
	No.2 Company.
	No.1 Company.
	Police.
	Rear Guard, 1 platoon No.1 Company.
5. HALT.	The Battalion will halt near VILLERS BRULIN ~~PENIN~~, orders with reference to the exact location will be issued to O.C. No.4 Company later. The march will be resumed at 4-0 p.m.
6. DESTINATION.	1st day. HOUVELIN & MAGNICOURT. Nos. 4 & 3 Companies will be billeted in MAGNICOURT. Guides will be at HOUVELIN to meet the Battalion. Orders for move on 21st May will be issued later.
7. REPORTS.	To O.C. Battalion with No.4 Company.
8. DETAIL.	Battalion Orders of 19th inst.

Major & Adjutant.
1st Provisional Garrison Guard Battalion.

DISTRIBUTION.

Copy No.	1,	O.C. No.1 Company.
"	" 2,	O.C. No.2 Company.
"	" 3,	O.C. No.3 Company.
"	" 4,	O.C. No.4 Company.
"	" 5,	Quartermaster.
"	" 6,	Transport Officer.
"	" 7,	Medical Officer.
"	" 8,	File.
"	" 9,	File.

SECRET.   NOT TO BE TAKEN INTO ACTION.

Appendix II

GENERAL INSTRUCTIONS FOR THE DEFENCE OF THE HAUTEVILLE SECTOR.

Reference, Sheet 51.c. 1/40,000.

LIMIT OF BATTALION SECTOR.
The Battalion has a definite sector of the reserve line to garrison, and to defend if necessary. This is divided into 4 Company sectors, No. 1, 2, 3 & 4 in this order from South to North, each Company having its own organisation in depth for defence, R.E. work, etc.

Southern limit (right flank) about half way between HAUTEVILLE and FOSSEUX.
Front line, P.4.d.8.6.   )
Line of resistance, P.4.d.3.8.) exclusive.
The limit is marked by definite points on the ground.

Northern limit (left flank) about 500 yards south of the village of LATTRE ST QUENTIN.
Front line, J.30.c.7.9.
Line of resistance, J.30.a.3.2.
The limit is marked by a communication trench which is included in the Battalion sector.

LIMIT OF COMPANY SECTORS.
No. 1 Company:-
From, southern limit of sector
    P.4.d.8.6. front line,   )
    P.4.d.3.9, line of resistance,) exclusive.
To, northern limit of sector,
    P.5.a.7.1. front line,   )
    P.5.a.9.5. line of resistance,) inclusive.
       (road junction)

The HAUTEVILLE-FOSSEUX Road marking the limit in each case.

No. 2 Company:-
From, northern limit of No. 1 as above, exclusive,
To, communication trench from line of resistance at J.35.d.4.2. to front line. This trench is the northern limit of this Company's sector (inclusive).

LIMIT OF COMPANY SECTORS (continued)

No.3 Company –
   From, northern limit of No.2 as above, exclusive,
   To, communication trench near windmill in J.35.b.6.9.
     (in line of resistance) to front line (exclusive).
     This trench marks the northern limit of this
     Company's sector.

No.4 Company –
   From, communication trench marking northern limit of
     No.3, inclusive,
   To, northern limit of Battalion sector in
     J.30.c.7.9. inclusive.

POSITION OF BATTALION H.Q. DUGOUTS, & AMMUNITION RESERVE FOR SECTOR & UNITS ON FLANKS.

There are five Battalion Headquarter dugouts in the Battalion sector either in course of construction or to be commenced shortly.
Position of our own Battalion Headquarters is at J.35.c.1.6.
Position of others for troops retiring on this line
   34.b.95.65.
   24.b.4.7.
   23.d.55.45.
One in support at 28.a.8.2.
The position of the Battalion main ammunition reserve is at J.35.c.1.7.
The unit holding the sector on the left or northern flank is the 4th Battalion R.Welsh Fusiliers,
        H.Q. LATTRE ST QUENTIN.
The unit holding the sector on the southern or right flank is the 5th Provisional Garrison Guard Battalion,
        H.Q. FOSSEUX.

Os.C.SECTORS.
O.C.Southern sector, Lt.Col.H.N.VINEN,
        H.Q. SOMBRIN.
O.C.Northern Sector, Lt.Col.E.H.THRUSTON,
     Training H.Q. LATTRE ST QUENTIN.
     Battle H.Q. AVESNES.

DISPOSITIONS. **No. 1 Company.** sector will be held as follows :—
Front line by 7 sections, with 7 posts of 1 section each.
Line of resistance by 2 platoons, with 8 posts of 1 section each.
The posts will be allotted positions so that the lines are more strongly held near HAUTEVILLE than towards the southern or right flank.
This sector will have an advanced post of 1 section at about P.5.d.1.3. on the edge of "horseshoe" wood.
This will also be a Military Police post.
The position of the Company H.Q. is at P.4.b.85.60.
If retirement is absolutly essential on this sector it will be carried out towards the village of HAUTEVILLE, not to the rear.

No. 2 Company. This sector will be held as follows :—
Front line by 7 sections, with 7 posts of 1 section each.
Line of resistance by 2 platoons, with 8 posts of 1 section each.
This Company will have an advanced post of 1 section at P.6.c.3.95. on the cross roads. This will also be a Military Police post.
The position of Company H.Q. is at P.5.a.8.8.

This Co will find a straggler post of 1 N.C.O. & 6 o.r. at J.26.d.4-3, for collection of stragglers ↓ to 9.4.92.

No. 3 Company. This sector will be held as follows :—
Front line by 7 sections in 7 posts of 1 section each.
Line of resistance by 2 platoons in 8 posts of 1 section each.
This Company sector will have an advanced post of 1 section at J.36.d.1.8. where the track meets the main road.
This will also be a Military Police post.
The position of the Company H.Q. is at J.35.d.50.85.

4.

DISPOSITIONS. No.4 Company. This Company sector will be held as follows:
(continued) Front line by 3 sections in 3 posts of 1 section each.
Line of resistance by 3 platoons in 12 posts of 1 section each.
This Company sector will have an advanced post of 1 section at 36.a.8.5. on the edge of the wood.
The allotment of posts will be with the object of holding the lines near HAUTEVILLE more strongly than towards the northern or left flank.
In case of retirement this will be towards the village of HAUTEVILLE, and not to the rear.
The position of Company H.Q. is at J.29.d.6.7.

BATTLE REGTL. The position of the Battalion R.A.P. is at J.35.c.5.7.
AID POST.

GENERAL. Two runners are detailed from each Company for communication with Battalion Headquarters. Their names should be known by all Company Officers.
Each section's post will be clearly marked in the trenches by a permanent mark in order that each section may be able to take up its position without hesitation.
Each Company will have definite lines of approach to the battle stations, these will invariably be followed, and will be taken when manning stations each morning.
These lines of approach should avoid the main roads.
Every man should know his position, and the route to be followed to get to it so thoroughly that he is able to take up his battle station without hesitation on a dark night.
The system of water supply in the trenches is as follows:-
This will be under Company arrangements.
There is a reserve of 2 - 50 gallon tanks at Battalion Headquarters, and 40 petrol tins will be available per Company for use in trenches.

INFORMATION. It is the duty of all Officers of the Battalion to obtain all information with regard to the defensive system of the sector in order to be able to give this information to troops retiring on the sector.

The following must be known :-

    Position of all trenches in the system -
        Front line.
        Line of resistance.
        Support Line.
        All C.Cs.
    All Battalion H.Q. dugouts in the sector.
    Position of ammunition reserve.
    Position of Aid Post.
    Position of advanced posts, & duties of advanced posts.

Organisation of Military Police.
    General dispositions of Battalion in battle stations.
    Points where good observation can be obtained.
    Ranges.

Names of all villages in the area, and where roads and tracks lead to.
    Water supply. Position of wells.
    Names and positions of woods.
    General duties of the Battalion as detailed in these instructions.

With the object of obtaining and imparting this information to all ranks under their command, Company Officers should study with a map -

    (1) Their Company sectors.
    (2) The Battalion sector.
    (3) The sectors north and south of the Battalion sector.

INFORMATION. (continued)	This should be done first with Platoon Officers and senior N.C.Os. Afterwards the platoons should be taken out and lectures given on the ground. The features of the country being pointed out to the men, and each man should be able to answer all questions with regard to the location of all principal points within the area. A good exercise will be to practise men in the attack of our lines in order to see things from the enemy's point of view. A detailed knowledge of the country in front is essential.
MAPS AND DIAGRAMS OF THE SECTOR.	1/40,000 sheets of the area are now available in Battalion Orderly Room for reference. 1/20,000 sheets of the sector and layered maps will shortly be available, and will be supplied to Officers as soon as possible. A large scale diagram of the defence system is available for each Company Commander on application.
DEFENCE OF SECTOR.	The main idea of the defence of the line is that it should be held in a series of strong points, or defended localities. These are generally the villages (in the case of the Battalion sector the strong point is the village of HAUTEVILLE). If these strong points are held it will be impossible - even if the enemy were to break through between them - for an advance to be made beyond the line. The chief object therefore is to hold the village at all costs, and the system of defence has been laid out with this object in view.

POSSIBLE CONTINGENCIES AND DUTIES IN ORDER TO MEET THESE CONTINGENCIES.

(1) In the event of an orderly retirement of our troops in front upon this line our duties are to be able to give Commanding Officers at once all information with regard to the defence system, and complete information with regard to the area of the Battalion sector as detailed in para. 2.

(2) In the event of a break through by the enemy in front of the sector the main object to be attained is to prevent confusion, to reorganise stragglers, and to ensure that our men shall not be influenced by reports from stragglers which are generally exaggerated and obtained from those who have seen confusion in some small section of the battle, and do not represent the true situation. Nothing is more infectious than confusion and panic, and it is our duty to prevent this taking place.

(3) In the possible event of a quick break through, and the line being attacked it will be defended by the Battalion, and the village of HAUTEVILLE held at all costs. There will be no question of retirement beyond the line unless ordered to do so by Brigade.

ADVANCED POSTS.

Localities the near edge of which are some 5 & 6 hundred yards in front of the general line of defence come under the heading of "advanced posts".

Advanced posts are not to form a definite line of defence. They are to hold up the attack until such time as this attack develops to such a point that it becomes necessary to fall back upon the troops in the rear in order to avoid being cut off. It is to decide when this retirement should be carried out that is the most difficult duty of the Officer or N.C.O. commanding an advanced post.

ADVANCED POSTS. (continued)

Cases have occurred in the present war when the enemy — taking advantage of confusion among retiring troops and the exaggerated rumours of strong enemy forces in rear which generally accompany any retirement which is not deliberate; — have gained strong positions with a very small force of men with machine guns.

Advanced posts, properly handled, will make it impossible for points of vantage to be gained near our lines in this manner.

DUTIES OF ADVANCED POSTS.

(1) To give information of what is occurring to the Company sector in rear. In misty weather it will probably be necessary to send out a patrol from the post.
(A good system of signalling by day and night is essential, and men should be detailed as runners to keep in touch with the Company sector in rear and carry reports.)

(2) To receive stragglers, organise them in parties, and march them to the Company sector in rear to be taken over by the nearest N.C.O.

(3) To fight until circumstances make retirement difficult, and then to fall back upon the Company sector.

Men for advanced post work should be carefully selected. It is their duty to prevent confusion being communicated to the troops in rear, and much depends upon their behaviour under trying conditions. They have a responsible position in keeping their sector informed without delay of all enemy movements to their front and flanks, and in ascertaining what is really the true state of affairs from reports brought in by stragglers.

GARRISON DUTIES.

These are :—

(1) R.E. work in completing the defence system
    (a) Trimming up trenches to ensure that men can fire over the parapet.
    (b) Draining trenches, and keeping sumps working.
    (c) Cleaning trenches from a sanitary point of view.
    (d) Making machine gun emplacements.
    (e) Completion of bombing straights.
    (f) Wiring and placing of obstacles, etc.

(2) Training.
    (a) Drill.
    (b) Physical exercises.
    (c) Musketry and signalling courses.
    (d) Lectures and tours to impart information with regard to the area.

GENERAL.

Besides R.E. work and training one of the principal duties is to create as soon as possible as high a standard of discipline as possible, and of physical fitness and esprit de corps in the Battalion.

In our special circumstances it is obvious that the most careful attention of all Officers should be directed to these points.

The Battalion is formed of men from many different units and who are not physically fit owing to wounds and illness, and have not worked together. There cannot at first be the cohesion and esprit de corps which is such an important point in obtaining the maximum efficiency in a fighting unit. These have yet to be created, and it is one of our principal duties therefore to do this as soon as possible. At the same time the comfort and amusement of the men should not be overlooked.

MILITARY POLICE.

The following men have been detailed from each Company for police duty, and will report to the Provost Sergeant when the order is received to man battle stations.

No.1 Company.	9236,	Pte.	Morley, H.
	42480,	"	Hogg, A.
No.2 Company.	26703,	"	Davies, W.J.
	200765,	"	Saunders, P.H.
No.3 Company.	38931,	"	McDonald, F.
	2430,	"	Parkinson, F.
No.4 Company.	424338,	"	McDonald, J.
	411277,	"	Carroll, P.

Rendezvous - gate of Chateau (near pond) map reference J.35.c.5.3.

Two men will then be detailed to proceed to each of the following points :-

(1) Where track meets road at J.36.d.1.9.
(2) Cross roads at P.6.c.4.9.
(3) Cross roads at J.35.a.8.1.
(4) Advanced post of No.1 Company at P.5.d.1.4.

DUTIES.

The duties of the police are:-

(1) To prevent stragglers from the front line from passing through our lines to the rear.

(2) To organise such men who are armed and equipped into parties and march them to the nearest Company sector. where they will be taken over by a N.C.O. in this sector. The police posts in the village will receive stragglers who are not armed and equipped from Company sectors, and report to Battalion Headquarters for instructions with regard to these men.

Company Commanders will take steps to see that no stragglers pass through their sector unless under command, and will make themselves acquainted with the position of the police posts.

MILITARY POLICE (continued)	They will hold all men who are armed and equipped within their sectors, and march others in charge of a N.C.O. in parties to the main police post in the village (at the chateau). They will, however, use their discretion as to whether such men should be retained in the trenches or sent back, the main object being to prevent confusion by keeping men who have lost their nerve under supervision and control.
RATIONS WHEN IN BATTLE STATIONS.	The following men have been detailed to report to the Quartermaster to carry rations to the trenches in the event of a prolonged period of duty in battle stations :- No.1 Company. 1 N.C.O. and 8 men. No.2 Company. 1 N.C.O. and 8 men. No.3 Company. 1 N.C.O. and 8 men. No.4 Company. 1 N.C.O. and 8 men.
GAS.	Box Respirators will always be worn at the "alert" when battle stations are manned. Rattles will shortly be provided and used in the trenches and at Company and Battalion H.Q. In the event of a gas shell bombardment Box Respirators will be put on in the affected area and rattles sounded.

T.W.T. Isaac Major
cmdg 1st Prov. G. G. Bn.

1/7 G Worcester R. P. 46
A.T.C. huntingdon
1/7 [illegible] breast My

Date		Summary	Remarks
1st		Church parade cancelled - rode q.s.41/19/10. Bath employed - Training + R.E. work - Training = Drill & Lewis gun. NEB:J. been Machine fire Camp Sgts J. McGovern, Registery, NcOr & Pr. B° in Camp at CLARQUES. in other time - R.E. work entails [?] a defence system of trem sites - Lewis emp° & which will be opened by the Bn in an emergency. Major R.J. INGLES. reported for duty & taken on strength.	Started 36 Drill service & g. s q. a 2. Off. OR
2.		Sunday. R.E. work. weather fine	
3.		Training & R.E. work. Training = Platoon Musketry Rep & Coy Drill with camera for NCOs & men in squadding. Lewis gun & Physical Training - Location in Camp - (C.F.) R.E. [illegible] as nowt. attacked RB. in the fire Ref. g.s.-2.22. Rev'd J. Bradley for a nowt. 2nd Lt. C BROWN. myself & 7r G. Bn B. Bray left Training & R.E. work. no before - Training as yesterday. Coms as yesterday 2 Lieut H.L HARRIS. reported for duty & taken on strength.	Off OR
4.			Off OR
5th		Training & R.E. work, no atm - Lewis no atm - location no store - weather fine	OR

A.F.C. 2118.
17th Gurwar B. Worcester Reg.
Month of June —

Date	Hour	Summary	Remarks
6th		Training & R.E. work as above. Courses as above. Location as above — weather fine — an alteration in programme of work of training received from Brigade Head Qrs. See appendix I G.S. 108/19/11 of 5.6.18. Thus to come in force tomorrow morning."	P/L
7th		R.E. work & Training — morning & evening respectively. Courses as above. Location as above — weather fine — 55 Privates arrived from Reinforcement Depôt. Strength on strength (P.B.).	P/L
8th		R.E. work & Training as above. Courses as above. Location as above — weather as above — weather fine —	P/L
9th		Sunday. Location as above — weather fine. Battalion marched to the Stations and inspection at 8.0 am. Brigade battle Head quarters closed down at 11.0 am. and Battalion returned to Camp —	P/L

17th Garrison Bn. Worcester Regt.
A.F.C. 2118.
Month of June

Date	Diary	Initials
10th	R.E. work. Trench digging. Training - Company, Platoon, Musketry & gas drill - Lewis Gun Training. Learn Gun Squadding & General classes of instruction. Location as above - weather fine morning - rain moderate afternoon.	P/L
11th	R.E. work & Training as above. Classes of Training as above. Location as above - weather fine.	P/L
12th	R.E. work & Training as above. Classes of Training as above. Location as above - weather fine - Brig: Gen: C.G. on day visit to 17th Bn. Worcs R. 17th Gar Bn. gave a letter on 17th Gar Bnt. R.	P/L
13th	R.E. work & Training as above. Classes of Training as above. Location as above - weather fine. Inspection by Maj. Gen. Pug. Comdg IX Corps.	P/L

WAR DIARY
or
INTELLIGENCE SUMMARY

(Erase heading not required.) 17th Div. 15th Worcester Regt.

Army Form C. 2118.

Place	Date	Hour	Summary of Events and Information	Remarks and references to Appendices
as above	14th		R.E. work & Training as above. Classes of Instruction as above. Weather fine.	
— do —	15th		Training as above. Classes of Instruction as above — Tactical exercise for Officers. Kit Inspection — Weather fine —	
— do —	16th		Sunday. Church Parade C of E — R.C. & Non-conformist — Warning order rec'd to move — B.A. 405 of 15th. To be prepared to march at 2 hrs. notice — 15th. Followed by B.A. 407 of 16th. Cavalry town & gun en terre to be concealed — with instructions "stand by" & await further orders.	
— do —	17th	5.30pm	Training as above. Classes of Instruction as above. Location as above. Weather fine — Movement order rec'd. To proceed to St Martin au Laërt Tomorrow morning.	Appendix II 176 Inf Bde No.112 of 17.10.18

WAR DIARY
or
INTELLIGENCE SUMMARY.
(Erase heading not required.)

Army Form C. 2118.

Place	Date	Hour	Summary of Events and Information	Remarks and references to Appendices
as above on march	18"	5.30am	Bt. moved - (Bt. operation order no 41 of 17th Jan. 1918	Appendix III
Salperwick Maps H.29.c. Sheets 27A S.E. R.21.c.7.0		11.0am	arrived at SS huts on dunes. Issued not by Staff Captain 121st Brigade & directed to proceed to (Salperwick) SALPERWICK - map ref:- Bt. in scattered huts nr. hd. 121st Brigade & 40th Division	
		2.0pm	H.Qr. of companies billeted 31 men fell out on march. Rear party h.t. returned at Cl. in quar — 2 officers 169 other ranks. also 1 officer killed - brother from Captain H.G. AYLMER transferred to 72.5 Ks Royal Dublin Fus.- Training:- Platoon section drill - Carriery of instruction. General Bry.	
— do —	19"	6.30pm	Course (no holiday transport day) - lewis gun - Signalling - Brig.	
— do —	20"	9.30am	Gen. 121st Bde. inspected the Bt. - another from. Training as above. Coming of Inst. as above - lecture from C.O. visited HAZEBROUCK - French System -	
— do —	21"		Training as above. Coming of Inst. as above - lecture from Company Commanders visited Hazebrouck trench system - reported 15th -	

Army Form C. 2118.

WAR DIARY
or
INTELLIGENCE SUMMARY.
(Erase heading not required.)

Instructions regarding War Diaries and Intelligence Summaries are contained in F. S. Regs., Part II. and the Staff Manual respectively. Title pages will be prepared in manuscript.

Place	Date	Hour	Summary of Events and Information	Remarks and references to Appendices
Recr 27A SE R.21.c.7.0.	3 22		Training as above. Course of Instruction as above — weather fine — 5 O.R. reinforcements reported for inst —	
		11.0pm	Movement order rec'd. — (121 Inf. Bde. O. B. N°20 of 22.6.18) —	Appendix IV
	3 23		In accordance with orders rec'd from 121st Bde — i.e. 121st Inf. Bde O.B. N°20 of 22.6.18. The Bn moved by bus from Calonguette to SAIPERWICK (less 1 battn) — WALLON CAPELLE (for spare bn when A°95 & 51.17.6.) (viz. B. Lancaster Regt.)	Appendix V
Recr 27A U.6.d.4.7.		4 pm 5.40pm	Entrained — Detrained — Bn encamped in fields at LE NOIR TROU & huts & bivouacs weather fine —	
U.6.d.4.7.	4 24		Training Specialist platoons & company drill — musketry & a.a. drill — Courses of Instruction as above — weather fine — gain of front — Major J. Macarthy D.S.O.M.C. — South Lancs Regt. arrived to take on tempory — 2nd in command 1 Ci-in-Chief inspected 121st Bde — did not see the Bn —	

Army Form C. 2118.

WAR DIARY
or
INTELLIGENCE SUMMARY.
(Erase heading not required.)

Instructions regarding War Diaries and Intelligence Summaries are contained in F. S. Regs., Part II. and the Staff Manual respectively. Title pages will be prepared in manuscript.

Place	Date	Hour	Summary of Events and Information	Remarks and references to Appendices
asylum	25.		In accordance with 12th Bde order the 13th received orders	Appendix VI
		10.30am	Officers in instruction appointed etc. in Hazebrouck — HAZEBROUCK trench system	
		3.0pm	13th bath in camp — breathe fine — 52 B & 763 O.R. sent away to baths — Kit inspection by O.C. T.M.B. — Major J. McCarthy-O'LEARY in orders today —	
Asylum	26		Discovery of wounded — course of instruction as usual — weather fine — C.O. with Company Commanders — carried out a reconnaissance in HAZEBROUCK trench system.	
Asylum	27.		13th received Battle Orders in HAZEBROUCK trench system. 13th went in instruction — No.2 & 4 companies — been on musketry firing — & not with 13th — weather fine — Captain C.J. POWER reported for duty, & taken over command of J.S.M. Coy.	

Army Form C. 2118.

WAR DIARY
or
INTELLIGENCE SUMMARY.
(Erase heading not required.)

Instructions regarding War Diaries and Intelligence Summaries are contained in F. S. Regs., Part II. and the Staff Manual respectively. Title pages will be prepared in manuscript.

Place	Date	Hour	Summary of Events and Information	Remarks and references to Appendices
Sheet 91 A SE. U 26 d 4.9. RENINGHELST	28.6.16		Coy training as usual. 9.0 a.m. -12.30 p.m & 2 p.m - 3.30 p.m training staff of 12th (S) Batt YORK. R. (2) arrived and taken on strength of the battalion. (see appendix VII). Lt. Col. A. W. Becher D.S.O. assumed command of the Battalion. Orders received for Battalion to be formed into a PIONEER Battalion and become PIONEER BATTALION 40th Division.	VII
"	29.6.16		Coy training as usual. Appointments as per appendix VIII appeared in orders.	VIII
"	30.6.16		Church Parade at 12 noon. Battalion Sports in afternoon and Evening. Prizes given away by Brig. Gen. W. B. GARNETT D.S.O. Commanding 121st Inf Bde.	

Williams Lt. Col.
Comdg. 17. G. Batt. WORCESTER R (P)

7th Bn WORCESTERSHIRE Regt. (P) Monday VIII

Extract from B.R.O. No 71 d/ 29-6-18.

6. Appointments:-

The following appointments are made with effect from 29-6-1918.

OFFICERS

Capt. T.K.G. Ridley to be Adjt. vice Major F.R.O'Kem
Lieut. R.O.Taylor - Lewis Gun Officer
  "   C.W. Hogg - Signalling Officer vice 2/Lt. E. Gamner
  "   E. McMahon. Quartermaster vice Capt. & McMahon
  "   T.L.C. Wood - Assistant Adjutant Gamner

O. RANKS

9468 R.S.M. Mourner - To be R.S.M. vice R.S.M. Davenport
200546 RQMS Mower, J. to be RQMS vice RQMS Church
19914 & SM Armstrong Q. to be & SM. To 2 boy. vice a/& S.M. J. L.
21207 BQMS Norman J. -- BQMS to 2 boy vice BQMS Ambrose
19912 &SM. Canham T.O, MM -- & S M. To 3 boy vice A/C/M Summers
19940 BQMS Featherstone, a.G --- BQMS Q 4/3boy vice Hanover
                            Holcey
19948 " Ferguson, a. -- BQMS vice BQMS Weedo

APPENDIX 14. WAR DIARY.

17th G. Bn. Worcs. Regt.
23rd G. Bn. Lancs. Fus.
17th G. Bn. R. Sussex Regt.
4th G. Bn. R.W. Fus.

G.S.108/19/1
5.6.18.

In continuation of previous instructions :-

1. Sunday will in future be the day on which no digging is carried out.
   Four hours training will be carried out, to be completed before 11.30 a.m. The remainder of the day will be given to the men for a complete rest.
   Voluntary Divine Services should be arranged for.

2. On all other days digging will commence at an early hour and will continue till tasks are finished. The heat of the day will be avoided for the one hour's training, which will take place between 5.30 and 6.30 p.m.

3. A statement of the Training to be carried out during the ensuing week will be forwarded to Battalions each Friday. Battalions will make no alteration to this without permission from Brigade Headquarters.

4. Every available Officer, N.C.O. and man will be employed on the digging except 100 men, who may be excused for training as specialists.
   Whenever the working strength of a Battalion falls below 600 O.R. a report will be rendered to Brigade H.Q. in explanation with Parade State as per attached pro-forma.

5. This office letter G.S.105/19/1 dated 4/6/18 is cancelled.
   Training programmes, showing training to be carried out on the following day, will be rendered to reach this office by 7 p.m. daily as previously.

(Sgd) R. Grant, Lt.
for Captain, Brigade Major.
176th Infantry Brigade.

5..6..18.

SECRET.   APPENDIX 2.   WAR DIARY.   Copy No. 3.

176th INFANTRY BRIGADE ORDER No. 112.

Ref. Maps. HAZEBROUCK, 5.a.;
27.a. Eastern Half, 1/40,000.;
36.d. 1/40,000.   June 17th, 1918.

1. The undermentioned Battalions will march to ST.MARTIN-au-LAERT Area to-morrow, 18th instant.
   Units will pass the Starting Point as follows :-

Unit.	From.	To.	Starting Point.	Time.	Route.
23rd G. Bn. Lancs.	BILQUES.	ST.MARTIN -au-LAERT	Fork Rds. F.17.a. 75.55.	5.30.am.	HELFAUT - GONDARDEMME - X - Rds.X.16.d.8.4. - X Rds. X.10.d.3.8.
17th G.Bn Worcs.R.	CLARQUES.	do.	X Rds. L.24.a. 00.10.	5.30.am.	X Rds. L.22.b.6.3. - thence due North via HELFAUT GONDARDEMME - X Rds. X.16.d.8.4. - X.Rds. X.10.d. 3.8.

   100 YARDS interval will be maintained between Coys. and between Battalions and their transport.

2. On arrival at ST.MARTIN-au-LAERT Units will come under orders of the 40th Division.

3. Billets in ST.MARTIN-au-LAERT will be obtained from the Area Commandant.

4. Completion of move to be wired to this Headquarters.

5. ACKNOWLEDGE by bearer.

                                    (Sgd) G.A.Taylor.
                                    Captain, Brigade Major.
                                    176th Infantry Brigade.

APPENDIX 14 — WAR DIARY.

17th G. Bn. Worcs. Regt.
23rd G. Bn. Lancs. Fus.
17th G. Bn. R. Sussex Regt.
4th G. Bn. R.W. Fus.

G.S.108/19/1
5.6.18.

In continuation of previous instructions :-

1. Sunday will in future be the day on which no digging is carried out.

   Four hours training will be carried out, to be completed before 11.30 a.m. The remainder of the day will be given to the men for a complete rest.

   Voluntary Divine Services should be arranged for.

2. On all other days digging will commence at an early hour and will continue till tasks are finished. The heat of the day will be avoided for the one hour's training, which will take place between 5.30 and 6.30 p.m.

3. A statement of the Training to be carried out during the ensuing week will be forwarded to Battalions each Friday. Battalions will make no alteration to this without permission from Brigade Headquarters.

4. Every available Officer, N.C.O. and man will be employed on the digging except 100 men, who may be excused for training as specialists.

   Whenever the working strength of a Battalion falls below 600 O.R. a report will be rendered to Brigade H.Q. in explanation with Parade State as per attached pro-forma.

5. This office letter G.S.105/19/1 dated 4/6/18 is cancelled.
   Training programmes, showing training to be carried out on the following day, will be rendered to reach this office by 7 p.m. daily as previously.

(Sgd) R. Grant, Lt.
for Captain, Brigade Major.
176th Infantry Brigade.

5.6.18.

SECRET. APPENDIX 2.   WAR DIARY.   Copy No. 3.

176th INFANTRY BRIGADE ORDER No. 112.

Ref. Maps. HAZEBROUCK, 5.a.
27.a. Eastern Half, 1/40,000.
36.d., 1/40,000.   June 17th, 1918.

---

1. The undermentioned Battalions will march to ST.MARTIN-au-LAERT Area to-morrow, 18th instant.
   Units will pass the Starting Point as follows :-

Unit.	From.	To.	Starting Point.	Time.	Route.
23rd G. Bn. Lancs.	BILQUES.	ST.MARTIN -au-LAERT	Fork Rds. F.17.a.75.55.	5.30 a.m.	HELFAUT – GONDARDEMME – X – Rds. X.16.d.8.4. – X Rds. X.10.d.3.8.
17th G. Bn Worcs. R.	CLARQUES.	do.	X Rds. L.24.a.00.10.	5.30 a.m.	X Rds. L.22.b.6.3. – thence due North via HELFAUT GONDARDEMME – X Rds. X.16.d.8.4. – X.Rds. X.10.d. 3.8.

100 YARDS interval will be maintained between Coys. and between Battalions and their transport.

2. On arrival at ST.MARTIN-au-LAERT Units will come under orders of the 40th Division.

3. Billets in ST.MARTIN-au-LAERT will be obtained from the Area Commandant.

4. Completion of move to be wired to this Headquarters.

5. ACKNOWLEDGE by bearer.

(Sgd) G.A.Taylor.
Captain, Brigade Major.
176th Infantry Brigade.

Appendix III

SECRET. Copy No. 11.

17th Garr. Battn. Worcestershire Regt.

OPERATION ORDER No. 41

17th JUNE 1918.

1. **INTENTION.** The Battalion will move tomorrow, the 18th inst. and will pass the starting point at 5.30 a.m.

2. **STARTING POINT.** Cross roads, L.24.a.00.10, where REBECQ – CLARQUES Road crosses road from THEROUANNE to CAUCHIE d'ECQUES.

3. **ROUTE.** Cross roads at L.22.b.6.3. (where REBECQ – CLARQUES road cuts THEROUANNE – INGHEM road) thence due North (middle road where three roads meet) to HELFAUT & CONDARDEMME; thence along main road to ST OMER to cross roads at X.16.d.8.4. thence North (left) to ST MARTIN au LAERT.

4. **ORDER OF MARCH.** The Battalion will march in the following order :-
   Headquarters Staff,
   No.1 Co.
   No.2 Co.
   No.3 Co. (less 1 platoon).
   No.4 Co.
   Rear guard — 1 platoon of No.4 Co.
   Rear party — 1 platoon of No.3 Co. 2 N.C.Os. & 25 men from each Company.

5. **DEFENCE.** See Battalion Standing Orders when on the move.

6. **HALT.** Near HELFAUT; exact location will be given later.

7. **REPORTS.** To O.C. Battalion at head of column, No.1 Co. Marching out states as soon as possible after passing starting point.

8. **DETAIL.** Battalion Orders of 17th inst.

(Signed) F.R. O'NEILL.
Major & Adjutant.
17th Garr. Battn. Worcestershire Regt.

DISTRIBUTION.
Copy No.1. Commanding Officer.   Copy No.7. Medical Officer.
     2. Major R.J. Ingles.   8. Transport Officer.
     3. O.C. No.1 Co.   9. Quartermaster.
     4. O.C. No.2 Co.   10. R.S.M.
     5. O.C. No.3 Co.   11. File.
     6. O.C. No.4 Co.   12. File.

File

SECRET.   Copy No. 7

121st INFANTRY BRIGADE ORDER No. 20

                                                    22nd June, 1918.

Ref. HAZEBROUCK Map 1/100,000.
     Sheet 27.A. S.E. 1/20,000
           27. S. W. 1/20,000
           36.A. N.W. 1/20,000

1.   The 121st Infantry Brigade will move by bus to-morrow, 23rd instant, in accordance with attached Table 'A'.

2.   All transport will move by road in accordance with Table 'B' attached and will march under the orders of O.C. No. 4 Company, 40th Divisional Train A.S.C.

3.   On arrival in the new area, units will be located as follows:-

    Brigade Headquarters   ...   C.3.c.5.3.
    2nd Garr.Bn. R.Irish R.   ...   U.27.c.3.2.
    23rd Garr.Bn. Lancs. Fus.   ...   U.27.b.3.5.
    23rd Garr.Bn. Cheshire R.   ...   U.27.a.0.3.
    17th Garr.Bn. Worcester R.   ...   U.26.d.4.7.
    No. 4 Coy., Divl. Train.   ...   U.28.b.2.6.

4.   Each battalion will detail one officer to report to an officer from Brigade Headquarters at cross roads R.26.d.6.8. at 2 p.m., when he will be given the lorries detailed for his battalion.

5.   Completion of moves and location of Headquarters will be notified to Brigade Headquarters.

6.   Brigade Headquarters will close at SALPERWICK at 2 p.m. and will re-open at C.3.c.5.3. at the same hour.

7.   ACKNOWLEDGE.

                                                    Captain,
                                                    A/Brigade Major,
                                                    121st Infantry Brigade.

Issued at 10.30 a.m.

        Copy No. 1 to G.O.C.
             2   Staff Captain.
             3   O.C. Bde.Signals.
             4   O.C. 2nd.Garr.Bn.R.Irish R.
             5   23rd Garr.Bn.Lancs. Fus.
             6   23rd Garr.Bn.Cheshire R.
             7   17th Garr.Bn.Worcester R.
             8   H.Q. 40th Divn(G).
             9   40th Divn(Q).
            10   A.D.M.S. 40th Div.
            11   O.C. No. 4 Coy. A.S.C.
            12   Supply Officer, 121 Bde.
            13   A.P.M., 40th Division.
            14   H.Q. 119th Inf. Bde.
            15   120th Inf. Bde.
         16-17   War Diary.
            18   File.

Table 'A' to accompany 121st Infantry Brigade Order No. 20.

Serial No.	Formation	From	To	Embussing Point	Debussing Point	Time of Embussing
1	Brigade Headquarters.	SALPERWICK	C.3.c.5.3.	R.26.d.6.8.	U.20.c.9.2.	2.0 p.m.
2	2nd Garr.Bn.R.Irish R.	TILQUES.	U.27.c.3.2.	R.25.b.5.6.	do	2.15 p.m.
3	23rd Garr.Bn.Lanc.Fus.	LONGUENESSE	U.27.b.5.5.	M.10.d.3.8.	do	2.15 p.m.
4	23rd Garr.Bn.Cheshire R.	TILQUES	U.27.c.0.3.	R.19.c.5.2.	do	2.15 p.m.
5	17th Garr.Bn.Worcester R.	SALPERWICK	U.26.d.4.7.	R.26.d.6.8.	do	2.15 p.m.

Table 'B' to accompany 121st Infantry Brigade Order No. 20.

Serial No.	Transport belonging to.	Starting Point.	Pass Starting Point.	Route.
1	No. 4 Coy. Divl. Train.	Cross Roads, R.33.d.4.1.	11.0 a.m.	M.4. - M.10. - ARQUES - EBBLINGHEM - WALLON CAPPEL.
2	Brigade Headquarters.	do	11.5 a.m.	M.4. - M.10. - ARQUES - EBBLINGHEM - U.20.a.9.2. - C.3.c.5.3.
3	2nd Garr.Bn.R.Irish R.	do	11.8 a.m.	M.4. - M.10. - ARQUES - EBBLINGHEM - U.20.a.9.2. - U.27.c.3.2.
4	23rd Garr.Bn.Lanc.Fus.	do	11.13 a.m.	M.4. - M.10. - ARQUES - EBBLINGHEM - U.20.a.9.2. - U.27.b.3.5.
5	23rd Garr.Bn.Cheshire R.	do	11.18 a.m.	M.4. - M.10. - ARQUES - EBBLINGHEM - U.20.a.9.2. - U.27.a.0.3.
6	17th Garr.Bn.Worcester R.	do	11.23 a.m.	M.4. - M.10. - ARQUES - EBBLINGHEM - U.20.c.9.2. - U.26.d.4.7.

SECRET

17th Garr. Batt. Worcestershire Regiment

OPERATION ORDER No. 5a

23rd JUNE 1918

1. OPERATION   These orders are in continuation of Operation Order No.5
   ORDER No.5.

2. MOVE   The move will be by busses or motor lorries.

3. BILLETS.   Billets will be vacated by 11.30 a.m.

4. RATIONS   a. Dinners will be at 12 noon outside billets.
                  b. The rations in bulk now in Coys. arranged for today's
                     cooking will be taken by Coys. in the lorries to
                     destination.

5. REAR PARTY.   See Battalion Standing Orders when on the march, page 8
                  2/Lt. C.J.P.Vanderstein has already been detailed to
                  command the rear party. No rations will be necessary.
                  The party will fall in with their Coys. at the embussing
                  point at 1.45 p.m.

6. MEN'S KIT   Full marching order with blankets. No rations will be
                  taken with kit.

7. EMBUSSING   Cross roads, R.26 d.6.8.
   POINT

8. LORRIES.   2/Lt. E.L.M.Tuck will report to an Officer from Brigade H.Q.
                  at the embussing point at 2.0 p.m. and take over the
                  lorries detailed for this Battalion.

9. EMBUSSING.   Companies and H.Q.,O.C. will report to the Adjutant at
                  the embussing point at 1.45 p.m., and will then be given
                  their marching out orders.

10. DEBUSSING   The Battalion will debuss at STAPLE and will march
                  therefrom to Stationary Camp U.26.a.4.7.

11. TOMORROW'S   Rations for consumption on 24th instant will be delivered
    RATIONS.   on arrival at new camp.

12. WATER   The BOOME BECQUE from U.21.d. to the HAZEBROUCK - ST
    SUPPLY   SYLVESTRE CAPPEL Road is an important source of water
                  supply, and must be protected from pollution.
                  The following precautions will be taken :-
                  a. No washing or bathing will be allowed in the stream.
                  b. No camp or horse lines will be permitted within
                     200 yards of the stream.
                  c. No baths or utensils used for washing allowed to drain
                     into the stream.
                  A.P.M. 40th Division will arrange for Military Police
                  to assist Traffic Police in this matter.

                                    (Signed) W.L.COX, Lieut.
                                             A/Adjutant
                                    17th Garr. Battn. Worcestershire Regiment.

SECRET.   R.S.M. appendix V

17th Garr. Battn. Worcestershire Regiment.

OPERATION ORDER No.5.

                                            22nd JUNE 1918.

Reference. HAZEBROUCK Map. 1/100,000.
            Sheet 27A. S.E. 1/20,000.
                  27J S.W. 1/20,000.
                  36.a.N.W.

1. INTENTION.   The battalion will move to LE NOIRE TROU tomorrow, where it will be accommodated in tents and trench shelters.

2. ADVANCE   2/Lt. J.Connell will be in charge of the advance party.
   PARTY.   He will meet at the Area Commandant's Office, ST MARTIN AU LAERT at 7.0 a.m. tomorrow the 5 lorries allocated to this Battalion, and will conduct them to the Quartermaster's Stores, will remain with them while they are loaded and during the journey until all kit is delivered and contents conveyed to camping ground at U.26.d.4.7.
                The advance party will consist of :-
                    a. Pioneer Sergeant.
                    b. Sgt. Trumpeter Mortlock, S.G.
                    c. The Band.
                    d. 1 N.C.O. and 4 men of the Sanitary   (To be
                       section, 4 pitboys and 1 H.Q.   (detailed
                       cook.   (by R.S.M.
                    e. 2 men per Company, to be detailed by Cos.
                They will take with them one dixie from No.1 Cd. and one from No.3 Co. together with the unused portion of tomorrow's rations.
                The advance party will parade under the Pioneer Sergeant at the Quartermaster's stores at 7.0 a.m. tomorrow, and will report to 2/Lt. J.Connell on his arrival there.

                The tents and shelters will be dumped at U.26.b.6.2. The lorries, conveying kit, etc, may be utilised after offloading for conveying tents and shelters to the camping site.

                Full advantage will be taken of the cover from view afforded by hedges and trees. Any tents not coloured must be covered with mud.

3. LOADING   A loading party will be detailed as follows :-
   PARTY.   2 men from each Company and 1 N.C.O. from Co. on duty
   and See   (No.2 Co.), and will report at Q.M.Stores at 7.0 a.m.
   below   and load stores, S.A.A., Lewis Guns and tapes on lorries; they will then proceed with one lorry to Battalion H.Q. and there load Orderly Room furniture and papers.

                                    (Signed) F.L.Connell, Lieut.
                                                     & Adjutant.
                                    17th Garr. Battn. Worcestershire Regt.

2.

4. **OFFICERS KITS.** Officers kits will be at Quartermaster's Stores at 7/0 a.m. tomorrow.

5. **AMBULANCE.** The horsed ambulance will collect sick as usual tomorrow morning, and will proceed independently to new area.

6. **TRANSPORT.** Transport will move by road in accordance with table attached, and will march under the orders of No.4 Co. 40th Divisional Train, A.S.C.
   a. Limbers will report to Cos. at 9.0 a.m. for loading at their disposal, and will then report at Battalion H.Q. at 10.0 a.m.
   b. G.S. wagons will be loaded at Q.M. Stores by 10.0 a.m.
   c. The Headquarters Mess Cart will report at Headquarters mess at 9.0 a.m., and after loading will report at Battalion H.Q. at 10.0 a.m.
   d. The water cart will report at Battalion H.Q. at 10.0 a.m.
   Transport Officer and Transport will proceed to starting point in ST MARTIN AU LAERT at R.33.d.4.1. where it will report to Divisional Train as above.

7. **LOADING PARTY.** The loading party will after loading advance transport load G.S. wagons.

8. **FURTHER ORDERS.** Further orders will be issued tomorrow, and will contain (inter alia) details as to man's kit.
   Ten dixies per Company and 4 for H.Q. Co. will be retained, as also unused rations, and not loaded on limbers.

(Signed) T.L.C.Mond, Lieut.
A/Adjutant.
17th Garr. Battn. Worcestershire Regt.

MARCH TABLE.

Serial No. 6.
Unit. 17th Garr. Bn. Worcestershire Regt.
Starting point. Cross roads R.33.d.4.1.
Pass starting point, 11.23 a.m.
Route, X.4. - X.10. - ARQUES - EBBLINGHEM - U.20.a.9.2 ; U.26.d.4.7.

SECRET.

Appendix V

17th Garr. Battn. Worcestershire Regiment.

OPERATION ORDER No.5a.

23rd JUNE, 1918.

1. OPERATION ORDER No.5.   These orders are in continuation of Operation Order No.5.

2. MOVE.   The move will be by busses or motor lorries.

3. BILLETS.   Billets will be vacated by 11.30 a.m.

4. RATIONS.
   a. Dinners will be at 12 noon outside billets.
   b. Tea rations in bulk and the dixies retained for today's cooking will be taken by Companies and H.Q.Co. to destination.

5. REAR PARTY.   See Battalion Standing Orders when on the march, para.9. 2/Lt. C.J.P.Vandersteen has already been detailed to command the rear party. No rations will be necessary. The party will fall in with their Coy. at the embussing point at 1.45 p.m.

6. MEN's KIT.   Full marching order with blankets. No rations will be taken with kit.

7. EMBUSSING POINT.   Cross roads, R.26.d.6.8.

8. LORRIES.   2/Lt. W.L.H.Tuck will report to an Officer from Brigade H.Q. at the embussing point at 2.0 p.m. and take over the lorries detailed for this Battalion.

9. EMBUSSING.   Companies and H.Q.Co. will report to the Adjutant at the embussing point at 1.45 p.m., and will then hand in their marching out states.

10. DEBUSSING.   The Battalion will debuss at U.20.a.9.2. and will march therefrom to destination at U.26.d.4.7.

11. TOMORROW'S RATIONS.   Rations for consumption on 24th inst. will be delivered on arrival in new area.

12. WATER SUPPLY.   The BOOKE BECQUE from B.21.d. to the HAZEBROUCK - ST. SYLVESTRE CAPPEL Road is an important source of water supply, and must be protected from pollution.
The following precautions will be taken,:-
   a. No washing or bathing will be allowed in the stream.
   b. No camp or horse lines will be permitted within 200 yards of the stream.
   c. No baths or ablution places are to be allowed to drain into the stream.

A.P.M. 40th Division will arrange for Military Police to assist Regimental Police in enforcing this order.

(Signed) F.L.E.Wood, Lieut.
A/Adjutant.
17th Garr. Battn. Worcestershire Regiment.

Appendix VI

121st Inf. Bde. No. 826/6(G).

Officer Commanding,

    2nd Garr. Bn. R. Irish Regt.
    23rd Garr. Bn. Lancs. Fus.
    23rd Garr. Bn. Cheshire Regt.
    17th Garr. Bn. Worcester Regt.

----

1.   Battalions will man the WEST HAZEBROUCK LINE to-morrow morning, 25th June, in accordance with Brigade Instructions No. 1. Troops to be in position by 10.30 a.m. and to remain so until visited by the Brigadier-General, and orders given to return to camp.

2.   Battalions are the only troops available for this practice; R.E. and Labour troops will not attend.

3.   The positions of Lewis Guns should be decided on, ranges taken and range cards prepared by gun team commanders and these charts should be kept in case they are required. All Lewis Gun Instructors will accompany battalions and generally supervise this work. Lewis Gun limbers will not be taken in ffront xxx of the reserve line. 22 magazines per gun will be taken into the line. Usual instruction should be carried out when gunners have nothing else to do.

4.   Ranges of various prominent objects will be taken and made known to the men who form the garrison in the vicinity of them.

5.   Fighting order with steel helmets and box respirators will be worn by all ranks.

                                      Captain,
                                     A/Brigade Major,
24th June, 1918.   121st Infantry Brigade.

Appendix VII

12th Battalion Yorkshire Regiment (P).

Nominal Roll of Officers posted to 17th Bn. Worcestershire Regt

RANK			Initials & Name.	
Substve	Temp.	acting		
Major	Lt. Col		H.W. Becher, D.S.O.	
		Major	T.H. Carlisle, D.S.O., M.C. RE	attached
		"	C.M. Southey	
		Capt.	A.C. Mildred	
		"	T.K.G. Ridley	
		"	W.N. Crosby, M.C.	
		"	H.N. Thomas	
		Lieut	C.W. Hogg	
		"	R.C. Taylor	
		"	G.A. Dixon	
		~6m	E. Mulhall	

Appendix VII

12th Battalion Yorkshire Regiment (P)

Nominal Roll of W.O's, N.C.O's and Men transferred to 17th Bn. Worcester Regt. (P)

REGT'L NO	RANK AND NAME	REGT'L NO	RANK AND NAME
9468	RSM Millner. W	20814	L.C. Black. R.J.
200546	RQMS Mawer J.C	25068	" Scaife. J.W
19914	CSM Armstrong. A.	20954	" Hislent. J
19933	" Hermiston. R.P	23941	" Smith. A.E
19912	" Banham. T.O	22593	Pte Bainbridge. R.
19940	CQMS Featherstone. A.E	46148	" Brooks. J
19948	" Ferguson. A.	19956	" Rycroft. H
21207	" Norman. J	21377	" Copeland. J
A2250	A/S/Sgt. Martin. G	20200	" Dawson. R.
20007	Sgt. Punn. W	46628	L.C. Gray. A
19006	" Knowles. W	25282	Pte Murphy. C
21445	" Jefferson. J	21378	" Miller. R.P
20205	" Payne. J	20884	" Collock. R.
20065	" Hight. D	22054	" Lannon. J.
22568	" Wilson. J.W	21052	" Rutter. H
23932	" Gillespie. W.A	21330	" Stephenson. C
46122	" Bruce. G	19949	" Shipper. W
15109	" Carney. T.	20812	" Trafford. T.
21047	Cpl Allinson. T.W	20972	" " J.W
22651	" McCarthy. C	19996	" Tate. T
20817	" Goodrum. H.L	20181	" Thompson. J
19493	" Bartell. J.A	19043	" Rodgers. C
47928	" Wright. E.G	34819	" Hardaker. E

Headquarters (a)
40th Division

[Stamp: 17th GARRISON BN., WORCESTERSHIRE REGIMENT. Date 2/8/18]

Hesworth War Diary for
July, 1918.

Cmdg 17th Bn Worcester Regt
Major
(Pioneers)

2/7/18

Army Form C. 2118.

WAR DIARY
17th Bn. Worcester Regt.
INTELLIGENCE SUMMARY.
(Pioneer)

(Erase heading not required.)

Instructions regarding War Diaries and Intelligence Summaries are contained in F. S. Regs., Part II. and the Staff Manual respectively. Title pages will be prepared in manuscript.

Summary of Events and Information   July 1918.

Place	Date	Hour	Summary of Events and Information	Remarks and references to Appendices
Aud BASE U 26 d 4.9 LE HAVRE	1.7.18		Capt Andrews, Cooper & Int. 9.0 a.m. to 12.30 p.m. & 2 p.m. to 3.30 p.m. Special classes in L.G. & Signalling continued.	
-do-	2.7.18	10.0 a.m	Rahotte inspected with 126th Inf Bn. by H.R.H. the Duke of CONNAUGHT K.G. K.T. K.P. &c. in field near SARCUS. Practice Parades held in morning on Rahotte. Parade formed. Coy Training continued. Special classes continued.	
-do-	3.7.18		Special class for N.C.O.s commenced under C.S.M. W.J CURREY H.G. Staff.	
-do-	4.7.18		Bn. shifted to Bn. at STAPLE	
-do-	5.7.18		" " " " "	
-do-	6.7.18		Ass Coft: & Q.M. games transferred to R.I.R.	
-do-	7.7.18	12 noon	Church Parade.	
-do-	8.7.18		Coy training continued. No 1 Coy & Pioneers under training fired on LAND R.R. No 4 Coy entrained and proceeded abroad into other line Companies 2/Lt JEFFREY & CONRAN transferred to A/G Ball. R.I.R., 121 Bde. Special chown entrained. Class of 15 men in SCOUTING commenced. C.A. Andrews and Burnwell Browne continued. T. Major J.H. Enbick D.S.A M.G.R.E. L.B. Roe.	
-do-	9.7.18		Maj. T.R. O'Neil & Lieut. E.W.L. Jowle to England, sick on 4th July. 2nd/Lt. Capt. C. Luddoch transferred to (2nd) 8th Batt. B.I.R., Capt. J.H. Baffle, 1.7.18 Moffat 1.7.18 Burngless, 2/Lt. G. Gunningham, 2/Lt F. Phillips, 2/Lt. A. Morrow, Maj. J.M. O'Leary also to 8th Bn. B.I.R. 2/Lt. A. Mandley, 2/Lt W. Sheppard, 2/Lt J.H. Blee, 2/Lt. H. Sharples from (10th Bn. Worcester Regt.).	
-do-	10.7.18			
-do-	11.7.18		Training continued to regimental classes as form 7d.	
-do-	12.7.18		Church Parade.	
-do-	13.7.18		Training continued.	
-do-	14.7.18		Occupation of trenches practised by No. 1 Coy.	
-do-	15.7.18		No. 2 & 4 Coys. musketry range practice /3 hours each on LA BELLE; HOTIESSE; range (C.2.2.c).	
-do-	16.7.18			
-do-	17.7.18			

Army Form C. 2118

WAR DIARY
11th Bn Worcester Regt.
INTELLIGENCE SUMMARY
(Erase heading not required.) (Pioneer)

Instructions regarding War Diaries and Intelligence Summaries are contained in F.S. Regs., Part II. and the Staff Manual respectively. Title Pages will be prepared in manuscript.

July 1918

Place	Date	Hour	Summary of Events and Information	Remarks and references to Appendices
Sheet 27A. SE.18 U.26.D.4.7	18/7/18	9.30am	No. 1 Coy moved to BORRE (W.13.d. central) with 119th Brigade who became attached to the 1st Australian Div. No. 2 & No. 3 Coy continued training as before.	
	19.7.18		No. 3 Coy continued training, Lewis gun class fired on LYNDE RANGE. No. 1 Coy engaged clearing near defence line at Headquarters. No. 2 & 3 Coys billeted at STAPLE.	at W.19.C.9.3.
	20.7.18		No. 1 Coy clearing trenches as y'day, clearing ground for D.H.Q. Baths at HAZEBROUCK, & railway R.E. material at BORRE SIDING.	
	21.7.18		No. 1 Coy " " " " " "	
	22.7.18		Remainder of Bn. attended Church Parade of Division (less 1 Brigade) near SERCUS, Dep. Ast. Chap. Gen. XV Corps. No. 1 Coy clearing trench etc at W.19.C.9.3 and W.19.d.6.4, clearing ground for Div. Baths etc. officiated. Cos. 2 & 3 Coys training.	
	23.7.18		Same as before.	
	24.7.18		No. 1 Coy commenced coy concrete floor in Baths, remainder continued training.	
	25.7.18		No. 1 Coy completed " " " " "artillery" bridge approach continued at HAZEBROUCK, rain interfered to some extent.	
			227. Co. H.W. BECHER D.S.O. attached to 9th batch. of 118th I.N. Staff Ct. 117 Bde.	
	26.7.18		No. 1 Coy continued " " " " 2 & 3 Coys continued training at N.H.Q.C. 2 & 3 Coys taken over by Major. R.B. INGLES taken on strength.	
	27.7.18		No. 1 Coy continued meeting, railway timber, & making wire crossing at 26.7.18	
			" " " " at BORRE J, HAZEBROUCK, y'day, leading respectively, also	
	28.7.18		Lewis gun firing at HONDEGHEM, & repairing roads at W.20.B.1.9 & W.21.C.4.9. 2 & 3 Coys continued training. Voluntary church parade at 2 pm in Battalion. 18 all ranks attended.	
	29.7.18		No. 2 & 3 Coys attached at the disposal of C.R.E. 40th Division for work on WEST HAZEBROUCK LINE.	
	30.7.18		No. 1 Coy attached to LE NOIR TROU. No. 2 & 3 Coys deepening & building W. HAZEBROUCK line from D.19.a.30.6 north.	
	31.7.18		No. 1 Coy working in camp on splints. Barbed wire length No. 2 & 3 Coys on trenches as y'day.	

R.A. Hughes, Major.
Cmdg. 11th Bn Worcester Regt.
(Pioneer)

Headquarters (A)
40th Division

[Stamp: 17th BN., WORCESTERSHIRE REGIMENT. No. W.D. Date 2-9-18]

Herewith War Diary
for the month of August.

M.B. Kirke
Lieut Colonel.
Cmdg. 17th Bn. Worcestershire Regt.
(Pioneers)

2/9/18

WAR DIARY
or
INTELLIGENCE SUMMARY

Army Form C.2118

17 Worcester Regt

Place	Date	Hour	Summary of Events and Information	Remarks and references to Appendices
WEST HAZEBROUCK	1.8.15		No 2 & 3 Coys continued deepening and drawing W. HAZEBROUCK LINE from 6.10 a.m. to 0.30. Battalions	
LA BELLE HOTESSE LE NOIR TROU	2.8.15		No 1 Coy on Camp fatigue in Splinter bombs proof. Hours and Bivouacs. Battalion moved into billets continued on W. HAZEBROUCK LINE No 1 Coy had all the work at 2 B.W. Battalion moved into Camp near LA BELLE HOTESSE. Camp was recently occupied by 15 N.V.L.I. Major H.F. SHEPPARD M.C. joined and appointed second in command vice Major 3/6/15 Lt Col H.W. BECHER 2nd from 12th STAFFS and took over command of the Battalion. Batt told on scheme of work in occupation of WEST HAZEBROUCK LINE	
LA BELLE HOTESSE CAMP	3.8.15		Batt continued on WEST HAZEBROUCK LINE in case of emergency. No 2 Coy employed in cutting Coll and hedge near MOB RECoui STATION masonry fences digging & cleaning drains	
	4.8.15		Church Parade at 2.30 p.m. 2/Lt W.R UMBDEN.(L) WALKER.CF (3Cy) WALKER. CF (3Cy) reported for duty.	
	5.8.15		Batt continued 3 platoons No 2 Cy & 2 platoons 3 Cy arriving ledge a from preparing to commence near STEENBECQUE. Serious No 1 Cy best improvement in WEST HAZEBROUCK LINE C.S.C. 15/15m 2 Cy. 1/platoon 3 Cy looking to B.N.1 Emplacements at 0.13 b.1.9 & C.16 b.15 & C.23 o.1.9	
	6.8.15		Batt continued Same as 5.8.15	
LA BELLE HOTESSE CAMP & CANAL B.S.	7.8.15		Batt continued Same as 5.8.15 Battalion went with camp vacated by 1st K.O.S.B. Batt bet cut Scheme of 10th K.O.S.B. to occupation of WEST HAZEBROUCK LINE in case of enemy offensive	
	8.8.15		Batt continued Same as 5.8.15 except 1 platoon 3 Cy completed and sufficiently & made to work near STEENBECQUE ST.M. buried of Ridge & open town in front of WEST HAZEBROUCK LINE M STEEN BECQUE ST.	
	9.8.15		Batt continued Same as 5.8.15	

Army Form C. 2118

WAR DIARY or INTELLIGENCE SUMMARY

(Erase heading not required.)

Instructions regarding War Diaries and Intelligence Summaries are contained in F.S. Regs., Part II. and the Staff Manual respectively. Title Pages will be prepared in manuscript.

Place	Date	Hour	Summary of Events and Information	Remarks and references to Appendices
A. BERLE HOTE 28E. E.21.a.b.5.	10.8.18		2 platoons No.2. Cy Completing wiring near STEEN BECQUE STATION. No 1 Cy. No 3. Cy & 2 No. 2 Cy. French Improvement on WEST HAZE BROUCK LINE.	
"	11.8.18		Church Parades & Baths.	
"	12.8.18		Cays working on WEST HAZE BROUCK LINE digging drains, clearing field of fire, wiring, Revetting & general repairs, One Section of 229 Field Cy R.E. with each Company assisting them.	
"	13.8.18 to 16.8.18		— do —	
"	17.8.18		— do — 2/Lt. T.T. HUMPHRIES disembarked for duty & posted to No 3 Cy	
"	18.8.18		— do —	
"	19.8.18		No work.	
"	20.8.18 to 22.8.18		Work continued on WEST HAZE BROUCK LINE. Section from 229 F. Cy R.E. withdrawn on 20.8.18. 2/Lt F.F. Goodwin (?) 2/Lt TASISMART. (3) 2/Lt AGHOLLAND (2) reported for duty 21.8.18	
"	23.8.18 24.8.18		Baths making. Baths allotted to Batt.	
D.2.C.q.1. Shut 36 A N.E. 20.000.	25.8.18	9.30 am	Batt relieved 12. K.O.Y.L.I. Pioneers 31st Divn. in the line. Cy H.Q. No 1. SWARTENBROUCK. E.14.d. 55. 25. No 2. LA MOTTE AUBOIS. D.30.D.2.2. No 3. PETIT SEC BOIS. E.9.a. 4.2. B. HQ at D.2.c.q.1. No 1A GONEWELE.	
"	26.8.18		Batt. Employed in repairing Roads. No 1. Cy. Repairing. Road from E.22.a.5.3 to BEAULIEU FARM. E.28.d. 6.2. & Road from E.28.a.8.3. to VIEUX BERQUIN. No 2. Cy repairing road BEAULIEU FARM to LA COURONNE. (Pl. 2. Cy supplied making pickets in wood. No. 3. Cy repairing & road from SAPPITAS CORVEE (E.15.a.7.8).5 PRESIDENT CROSS. (E.14. C.9.3) — road from KELT CROSSING E.9.a.2.4. through GRAND SEC BOIS. & road from POINT CROSS (E.8.C.55) Northwards. (not Shelf 36A N.E. 1/20,000).	
"	29.8.18		No 1.Cy 3 platoon 2 Cy & 2 pl. 3. Cy repairing Roads. Remainder on Parade.	

Army Form C. 2118

WAR DIARY
or
INTELLIGENCE SUMMARY
(Erase heading not required.)

Instructions regarding War Diaries and Intelligence Summaries are contained in F.S. Regs., Part II. and the Staff Manual respectively. Title Pages will be prepared in manuscript.

Place	Date	Hour	Summary of Events and Information	Remarks and references to Appendices
D.Q.G.Q. Sheet 36A N.E. 1/20,000	28.9.18		Ref. Sheet. 36A N.E. 1/20,000. Battalion repairing following roads. ELK FARM to BEAULIEU FARM, RUE du BOIS. BEAULIEU FARM to LA COURONNE. SANITAS CORNER to PRESIDENT CROSS road. Road through GRAND SEC BOIS.	
"	29.9.18		- do -	
"	30.9.18		Batt. clearing following roads. main Road from PRESIDENT CROSS to VIEUX BERQUIN. RUE du BOIS Road. Road from BEAULIEU FARM to LA COURONNE. GRAND SEC BOIS Road.	
"	31.8.18		Batt. clearing following roads. main Road from PARADISE INN to LA COURONNE. Road from LA COURONNE to BLEU Road from VIEUX BERQUIN to LABIS FARM. RUE du BOIS road.	
			Strength at beginning of month. Off. 26. O.R. 803. End 33. 770.	
			Casualties Killed nil nil Wounded nil nil " Gas Sick 1. 23 die Causes . 19 9. 9.	
			Drafts Received. 9.	

W. Wilkes
Lt. Col.
Comdg. M.H. 102 C.R. (?)

1875 Wt. W593/826 1,000,000 4/15 J.B.C. & A. A.D.S.S./Forms/C. 2118.

Headquarters (A)
40th Division

Herewith War Diary for
the month of September

M.W. Rickets
Lieut Col
Cmdg. 17th Bn Worc Regt (Pioneers)

2.10.8

Army Form C. 2118

17 Worcestershire Regt

WSR B 24

WAR DIARY
or
INTELLIGENCE SUMMARY
(Erase heading not required.)

Place	Date	Hour	Summary of Events and Information	Remarks and references to Appendices
D.2.c.9.1 Ref map 36A Mussos	1.9.18		Battalion working on road from F.13.a.7.3. to HAUTE MAISON F.14.d.33. Clearing mud from roads & filling in shell holes. Ref map 36A N.E. 1/20000.	
"	2.9.18		No.1. Cy. armed being Bringers & bricks at F.21.b.1.8. ref map 36A N.E. 1/20000 " 2 " " " " " F.14.c.3.4. " 3 " " " " " F.13.d.7.6.	
"			Work on roads continued.	
PETIT SEC BOIS	3.9.18		HQ and transport moved to PETIT SEC BOIS. F.9.0.4.8. Cys working on filling in roads. No 1. Cy. from PONT WIJDAN to DOULIEU. No 2 Cy on approaches to bridges at HAUTE MAISON. No 2 Cy from CUTLET CORNER to PONT WEMEAU.	
"	4.9.18		No 3 Cy working on roads EAST of HAUTE MAISON BRIDGE to PONT WEMEAU. No 2. Cy from X roads in LE VERRIER towards STEENWERCK. No 1 Cy from LE VERRIER to DOULIEU. No 2 Cy moved to DOULIEU. F.3.a.5.8.	
"	5.9.18		No.3. Cy repairing road from HAUTE MAISON BRIDGE F.14.d.33. to CUTLET CORNER F.21.a.5.5. No 1. Cy repairing road from CUTLET CORNER EASTWARD. No.2 Cy repairing road from CUTLET CORNER past TIGER FARM to PONT WEMEAU & DOULIEU.	
"	6.9.18		- do -	
"	7.9.18		- do -	
"	8.9.18		- do -	
"	9.9.18		- do -	
"	10.9.18		No.1. Cy repairing road from CUTLET CORNER EASTWARD. No.2. Cy repairing road from PONT WEMEAU thro' LE VERRIER to WINE COTTAGE. No 3 Cy repairing road from CUTLET CORNER to DOULIEU.	

WAR DIARY or INTELLIGENCE SUMMARY

Army Form C. 2118

Ref. Map. MERRIS. Edition 2A.
Scale 1/20,000.

Place	Date	Hour	Summary of Events and Information	Remarks and references to Appendices
PETIT SEC BOIS E.20.4.3.	11.9.18		No 1 Coy advancing head from LE VERRIER toward DOULIEU to L.5.a.0.0. No 2 Coy from F.16.d.2.7. to PONT MENEAU. No 2 Coy from PONT MENEAU to LE VERRIER. " " from WINK COTTAGE to WINK STEENWERCK. Work stopped at 1.0 p.m. owing to heavy rain.	
"	12.9.18		No 1 Coy same as 11.9.18. No 2 Coy. from WINK COTTAGE through STEENWERCK. No 3 Coy same.	
"	13.9.18		No 1 Coy same as 11.9.18. No 2 Coy same as 12.9.18. No 3 Coy advancing road from LE VERRIER to ROSSIGNOL FARM.	
"	14.9.18		No 1 Coy advancing road from F.16.a.8.7. to PONT WEM EAU. No 2. o 3. Coy same as 13.9.18.	
"	15.9.18		– do –	
"	16.9.18		No 1 Coy No 3 Coy advancing road from LE VERRIER to LE PETIT MORTIER. No 2 Coy repairing road through STEENWERCK towards TROIS ARBRES. No 3 Coy round to TALLY FARM. A.21.C.u.5. through H.G. SHEPPERD came to temp. (cont).	
ONYX HOUSE N. STEENWERCK R.16.L.q.2.	17.9.18		H.Q. moved to ONYX HOUSE N. STEENWERCK. Transport moved to field at R.22.a.2.7. No 1 Coy 1 platoon advancing road from STEENWERCK to TROIS ARBRES. No 2 Coy same as 16.9.18. No 2 Coy 1 platoon advancing road from LE GRAND SENOMART. 12.29.a.4.8. towards LE KIRZEM. No 2 Coy advancing road from A.15.c.3.2. A.a.4 d.2.0.	
"	18.9.18		No 1 Coy moved to D.22 & 9.5. Work continued as in 19.9.18. No 6 platoon of No 1 Coy of same as 19.9.18. No 3 Coy proceeded to LA MOTTE to with work party Coy w. WIEZNE FOR G.T.	
"	19.9.18		No 1 Coy No 2 Coy same as 19.9.18. No 2 Coy 2 platoon on road R.19.a.1.3 to B.19.a.31. 2 platoon R.14.a.11 to A.20.b.6.0.	
"	20.9.18		No 1 & 2 Coy. Same as 19.9.18. No 3 Coy 1platoon on road from 3 platoons on road R.18.d.1.3 to R.25.a.6.2. A.24.a.11. to A.20.b.8.2.	

Major R.J. INGLES. Proceeded to LABOUR CORPS. Base Depot. Boulogne (S.o.S.)

WAR DIARY or INTELLIGENCE SUMMARY

Army Form C. 2118

Ref. War. MERRIS. Ed 2 A. 1/20000 & 36. (Scale 1/1000)

Instructions regarding War Diaries and Intelligence Summaries are contained in F. S. Regs., Part II. and the Staff Manual respectively. Title Pages will be prepared in manuscript.

Place	Date	Hour	Summary of Events and Information	Remarks and references to Appendices
ORY HOUSE N. STEENWERCK A.16.d.9.2.	21.9.18		No. 1 Cy. repairing road from LE VERRIER to LE PETIT MORTIER. No. 2. Cy. repairing road from GRAND BEAUMART to through LE NIRLEM towards LE PETIT MORTIER. No 3 Cy. repairing road B.19.a.31. to H.1.b.5.9. 1 platoon No. 1. Cy. taking down camouflage along road H.1.b.5.9 towards ORVILLE JUNCTION. B.29.a.3.8.	
"	22.9.18		— do — No. 2. Cy. found mess huts & billets at RIG FARM. A.30.a.5.b. 1 ∞ Q.M. MULHALL returned from hospital No. 1. Cy. Same as 21.9.18. No. 3. Cy. pushing ↑ inspection etc. 2/Lts. DONALDSON, BURGOYNE & FAWCETT, W.M. returned from Base	
"	23.9.18		No. 1. Cy. repairing roads from LE VERRIER & LE PETIT MORTIER. from G.W.A.31. to G.10. Crossroad from DIPPER B.1 to G.4.b.1.5. 1 platoon repairing camouflage along road H.1.b.5.9 towards ORVILLE TURNING No. 2 Cy. repairing road from WAR FARM. A.29.d. to LE PETIT MORTIER. No. 3. Cy. repairing roads H.1.b.5.9. to B.8.10.a.3.1. W. Captain B. ROBERTSON R.A.M.C. Ceased to be M.O. i/c of the Battalion. Captain C. TROUNCE. R.A.M.C. appointed M.O. i/c.	
"	24.9.18		No. 1. Cy. Same as 24.9.18. two platoons erecting camouflage at night No. 2. Cy. pulling & moving to A.29.0.5.1. PETIT MORTIER. old which nearly shelled. No. 3. Cy. repairing roads H.1.b.5.9 towards ORVILLE JUNCT. & road H.1.b.5.9 to A.24.c.9.5. & road A.19.a.31. to A.19.b.5.5.	
"	25.9.18		No. 1. Cy., Baths, & kit inspection etc. No. 2. Cy. Same as 24.9.18. No. 3. Cy. Same as 25.9.18.	
"	26.9.18		No. 1. Cy. erecting camouflage along road H.1.b.5.9 to ORVILLE Junct. a thing in creation at B.22.d.9.0. Repairing road G.b.a. to G.10 Crossrd. No. 2. Cy. repairing road through LE PETIT MORTIER. 1 platoon clearing STEEN BEC RIVER by debris working from DIPPER BRIDGE NORTHWARDS. No. 3. Cy. Repairing strong roads YELLOW CROSSING via OUL FARM to NIEPPE. YELLOW CROSSING to LE VEAU to B.7.a.9.5.	
"	27.9.18		— do —	
"	28.9.18		— do —	
"	29.9.18		No. 2. Cy. Release to road from B.7.a.9.5. through LE YEAU OUL FARM to NIEPPE & repairs to road leading to A.30.b.6.9. No. 3. Cy. Same as 27.9.18. No. 1. Cy. Same as 27.9.18.	
"	30.9.18		— do —	

Army Form C. 2118

WAR DIARY
or
INTELLIGENCE SUMMARY
(Erase heading not required.)

Instructions regarding War Diaries and Intelligence Summaries are contained in F.S. Regs., Part II. and the Staff Manual respectively. Title Pages will be prepared in manuscript.

Place	Date	Hour	Summary of Events and Information	Remarks and references to Appendices
			Strength.	
			Strength at beginning of month. Off. 33 OR. 770.	
			End — 34 715.	
			Casualties. Died of wounds. —	
			Wounded. 3	
			Evac. Sick. 60	
			Other Causes. 2/2 2/66	
			Drafts Received. 3 2/9 from Base	
			from Hospital.	
			29.9.18	
			Remarks. Major C.W. SOUTHEY granted 1 months leave. 2/Lt. DONALDSON took over command of 1 Coy.	
			W.W.Neilson Lt. Col.	
			Comdg. 14th 100 Re. B.(?)	

Headquarters (A)
    40th Division

    Herewith War Diary
for this Battalion for the month
of October 1918.

                                  Lieut. Col.
    Cmdg. 17th Bn. Worcestershire Regt. (Pioneers)

2.11.18

17th BN., WORCESTERSHIRE REGIMENT.
No.
Date 2.11.1918

Army Form C. 2118

WAR DIARY or INTELLIGENCE SUMMARY
(Erase heading not required.)

Ref. map. 36 NW 1/20,000. 40 DIV

25

Place	Date	Hour	Summary of Events and Information	Remarks and references to Appendices
BILLY-HOUSE Nr STEENWERCK A.16.a.2.9.	1.10.18.		No 1. Cy. repairing road from PETIT MORTIER to G.10. Central & road from H.1.b.5.9. to ORVILLE JUNCT. Erecting camouflage along road from H.1.b.5.9. to B.28.b.2.7. filling in crater at B.22.d.9.0. No 2. Cy. Clearing STEEN BECQUE RIVER of debris & repairing road through LE PETIT MORTIER to G.3.a.6.9. 1 Platoon No 2. Cy. attached to C.R.E. making track boards in NIEPPE FOREST. No LA MOTTE. No 3 Cy. repairing roads from B.7.d.9.5. through LE VEAU past our FARM to NIEPPE. & road from B.25.c.8.6 to A.30.a.4.9.	
"	2.10.18.		No 1. Cy. repairing road from H.1.b.5.9. to ORVILLE JUNCT. Road from B.29.c.3.6. to RIVER LYS. & Crater at B.22.d.9.0. No 2. Cy. repairing road from CROIX DUBAC towards H.1.b.5.9. Completed clearing STEEN BECQUE RIVER. 1 Platoon No 2. Cy. repairing road in LA MOTTE. No 3 Cy. repairing road from B.7.d.9.5. LE VEAU to NIEPPE & road from B.7.d.9.5. to B.8.a.8.9.	
"	3.10.18.		No 1. Cy. same as 2.10.18. No 2. Cy. repairing road in PONT DE NIEPPE to Railway at B.28.a. No 3. Cy. repairing roads from NIEPPE & roads to B.11.c.2.1. & to B.5.b.5.8. Main road from B.8.a.7.7. to NIEPPE. Heavy debris from fallen houses on roads in NIEPPE & PONT DE NIEPPE. No 3. Cy. moved to B.7.d.7.4. No 2. Cy. moved to B.9.c.6.4.	
"	4.10.18.		No 1. Cy. repairing roads from B.29.C.3.6. to RIVER LYS & road from ORVILLE JUNCT. to crater (mill) in PONT DE NIEPPE. No 2. & No 3 repairing roads same as 3.10.18. No 3. Cy. Same as 3.10.18.	
"	5.10.18.		Same as 4.10.18. No 1. Cy. moved to B.23.C.8.3.	
"	6.10.18.		No 1. Cy. repairing roads from B.29.C.3.6. to RIVER LYS. Road from PONT DE NIEPPE to NIEPPE. Road from B.28.b.2.8. to PONT DE NIEPPE. No 2. Cy. repairing roads C.7.b.5.1. to C.7.b.45.80. end 44 render to C.7.c.9.2. & C.14.a.3.5. C.14.a.b.0. No 3. Cy. repairing roads B.10.d.9.5. to B.11.b.0.2. to B.12.a.5.4. HQ & transport moved into VEAL HOUSE. H.1.b.7.9. & surrounding buildings & stables.	
VEAL HOUSE H.1.b.7.9.	7.10.18.		No 1. Cy. same as 6.10.18. No 2. Cy. repairing roads C.7.b.5.1 & C.13.b.9.4. Completed filling in 3 long craters. No 3. Cy. repairing Road B.5.C.35.50 to B.11.b.0.3 & road from B.5.C.35.50 to B.4.a.8.2. No 3. Cy. moved to NIEPPE B.16.a.7.4.	

1875 W. W393/826 1,000,000 4/15 J.B.C. & A. A.D.S.S./Forms/C.2118.

WAR DIARY or INTELLIGENCE SUMMARY

Army Form C. 2118

Ref. Maps 36 NW 1/20000

Place	Date	Hour	Summary of Events and Information	Remarks and references to Appendices
WEAL HOUSE A.16.c.7.9.	8.10.18		No 1 Cy. repairing road from B.29.c.3.6. to RIVER LYS (completed). Repairing road from Railway Crossing 18.22.b. to PONT DE NIEPPE (completed). Repairs to MAIN NIEPPE - PONT DE NIEPPE road in progress. No 2. Cy repairs to roads as follows in progress C.14.a.9.9. to C.9.c.9.3. - C.7.b.5.1. to C.1. central. Road from C.7.b.5.1 to C.14.a.9.9 via C.8.a.7.9 & C.8.a.9.4. & road from C.13.b.9.4. to C.14.a.9.9. to PONTOON BRIDGE on RIVER LYS at C.21.d. No 3. Cy. repairing roads B.S.a.35.50 to B.11.b.03. & B.S.a.35.50 to B.10.d.9.6. 2/Lt. W. SHRIMPTON joined from Base and posted to No 3 Cy.	
"	9.10.18		No 1 Cy repairing road from ORVILLE JUNCT B.29.c. to TOURGET PARMENTIER & road from ORVILLE JUNCT. to Railway Junct B.28.b. other two platoons No 1 Cy. No 3 & 2 Cys. Same as 8.10.18. Same as 9.10.18. 2nd Lt. W. SHRIMPTON joined & posted to No 3. Cy.	
"	10.10.18			
"	11.10.18		No 1 Cy. 2 platoons repairing ORVILLE Junct - PONT DE NIEPPE Road Rpl. No 1 Cy. & No 2 Cy. repairing main road from 11.8 central towards ARMENTIERES. No 3 Cy. building [illegible] from main [illegible] ARMENTIERES Road.	
"	12.10.18		No 1 Cy. Same as 11.10.18. No 2 Cy. repairing Same as 11.10.18. No 3. Cy. lays at ERQUINHEM & R.E. inspection. No 1 Cy moved to THUNDER COTTAGES A.28.a.3.8. 2/ Lt PEAKING joined & posted 1 Cy.	
"	13.10.18		No 1 Cy. Same as 11.10.18. No 3. Cy. 2 platoons repairing main ARMENTIERES road. No 2. Cy. Battle & kit inspection. & repairing road from RIVER LYS through PONT DE NIEPPE to NIEPPE.	
"	14.10.18		No 3 Cy Same as 13.10.18. No 2 Cy. repairing main ARMENTIERES road. No 1 Cy. baths & kit inspection.	
"	15.10.18		No 1 & 2. Cys repairing Road from B.30.c.4.2. through ARMENTIERES to CHAPELLE D'ARMENTIERES 1.8.b.2.2. No 3. Cy. completing roads in ERQUINHEM. NIEPPE & PONT DE NIEPPE. No 1 Cy moved into billets in ARMENTIERES C.26.d. No 2. Cy moved to H.S.B. central, [illegible] [illegible] [illegible] posted to Cys.	
"	16.10.18		No 1 Cy. Same as 15.10.18. No 2. & 3. Cy. Same as 15.10.18. No 3.Cy moved to ARMENTIERES. C.26.d. ARMENTIERES to HOUPLINES.	
"	17.10.18		No 1 Cy. Same as 15.10.18. No 2 Cy. repairing road from HOUPLINES to C.30. central filling in craters at C.30. central. & S.4.c.5.b. Roads due in fair condition except for craters and shell hole.	

WAR DIARY
or
INTELLIGENCE SUMMARY

Army Form C. 2118

Ref. Maps 36 N.W. 1/20,000. & 36. N.E. 1/20,000.

(Erase heading not required.)

Place	Date	Hour	Summary of Events and Information	Remarks and references to Appendices
WERL HOUSE. H.1.b.9.9.	19.10.18		No 1. Cy repairing road from HOUPLINES to PERENCHIES. filling in craters at c.30 central. No. 2 Cy filling in craters in VERLINGHEM. J.4.c.5.6. & at J.8.a.0.4. & repairing road from J.8.a.0.4. to J.4.c.6.6. No 3 Cy filling in craters at LA CROIX J.4.b.2.8. LA CROIX AU BUIS D.20.d.5.9. FONQUERAU D.2.b.c.1.4. No. 2. Cy moved to VERLINGHEM. No. 3.Cy to FME DUTAS. D.29.L.6.2.	
N° FORT du VERT GALANT D.29.b.5.6.	19.10.18		No 1. Cy completed crater at c.30 central at FONQUERAU. Craters at LA CROIX AU BOIS rARRAS FARM in progress. No 2 Cy " in PERENCHIES. Craters at LA CROIX & VERLINGHEM in progress. No 3 Cy filling in craters at D.29.b.9.6. D.24.c.5.3. D.24.c.5.2.0. E.25.a.8.5 (in WAMBRECHIES). H.Q. and transport moved to billets near FORT DU VERT GALANT. No 1 Cy moved to D.24.c.6.2.	
"	20.10.18.		No 1. Cy filling in craters in WAMBRECHIES at E.26.d.9.1. E.29.c.3.2. & clearing debris from streets. No 2. " Nr. FORT CARNOY. D.30.a.27. in VERLINGHEM. J.4.b.7.8. at ARRAS FARM (completed) & clearing road from PERENCHIES to VERLINGHEM. No. 3. Cy filling in crater at junct of road & Rly at D.24.c.2.0 (completing) E.25.c.8.5. D.24.c.5.3. & in WAMBRECHIES. H.1.b.9.3.	
"	21.10.18		No 1. Cy same but filling craters at E.29.c.5.9 in addition. No. 2 Cy same. No. 3. Cy same. All craters practically completed. Work handed over to Road Construction Cy R.E.	
MOUVAUX F.2.b.6.1.9.	22.10.18		No 1. Cy filling in craters at E.29.c.5.9. E.29.c.3.2. & E.29.b.9.7. E.26.d.9.7. No 2 Cy clearing road from L.1.a.0.9 to L.1.b.6.5.9 & from F.2.c.a.2. to L.1.b.0.9. No. 2. Cy moved to near MOUVAUX F.2.b.6.1.9. No 3. Cy moved to near LA MONIVEL. L.1.a.1.9.	
"	23.10.18		No 1. Cy same as 22.10.18. No. 2. Cy same. No 3 Cy resting and cleaning up. H.Q. & transport moved to MOUVAUX F.26 b.6.9.	
"	24.10.18		No 1. Cy same as 22.10.18. No 3 Cy continued No. 2 Cy work. No. 2 Cy baths, kit inspection etc.	
"	25.10.18		No 1. Cy same as 22.10.18. No 2 Cy continued work commenced on 22.10.18. No. 3 Cy baths. etc.	
"	26.10.18		Cap. Reskins	

WAR DIARY
or
INTELLIGENCE SUMMARY.
(Erase heading not required.)

Army Form C. 2118.

Ref. Map. Sheet 39 1/40,000.

Place	Date	Hour	Summary of Events and Information	Remarks and references to Appendices
LANNOY	27.10.18	14.00	The Battn. moved by road nord through ROUBAIX and relieved 15th Bn K.O.Y.L.I. Pioneers. 31st Division at LANNOY.	
"	28.10.18	10.15	No. 1 Coy moved into billets in LEERS NORD. Nos. 2 & 3 Coys moved into billets in NECHIN. HQ & transport remained at LANNOY.	
"	29.10.18		The Battalion lines transport inspected at NECHIN by Major Genl Sir W.E. Peyton K.C.B. K.C.V.O. D.S.O. Commanding 40th British Division. He expressed himself very well pleased with the work of the Battalion during the last three months & stated that he had received many congratulatory messages from its Army & Corps Commanders on its work the Battalion had done. 2 Platoon No. 1 Coy repairing road from A.B.a 16 PEC Q. Lt. Cox (1 Coy) & Lt. Tolson (3 Coy) finished. Company training in morning. Games in afternoon.	
"	30.10.18		—do—	
"	31.10.18		Strength at beginning of month. Offs. 33. O.R. 713 End " " 32. 703. Drafts Received — — Casualties Killed — 1 Wounded — 1 Gas (Sick) 1. 32 2/Lt HARRIS Transfers 4 2/15 CLEE 2/Lt VANDERSTEEN to 23 Lanc. Fus. 2/Lt SHARPLES Other Causes 3 1013.E.L. LANE 2/Lt ASHTON to 15. K.O.Y.L.I.	Offs. 6R 24. Base. 4. 2. 2/Lt Lt COX Lt. TOLSON. 2/Lt PERKINS 2/Lt SHRIMPTON. MWebber, Lt. Col. Comdg. 17th WORC. R. (P)

40P.

> 17th BN.,
> WORCESTERSHIRE
> REGIMENT.
> No. ....
> Date 3.12.18

Headquarters (A)
40th Division

Herewith War Diary for this Battalion for the month of November, 1918.

[signature]
Lieut. Col.
Cmdg. 17th Bn. Worc. Regt. (Pnrs)

3.12.18.

17 Worcester R.

Army Form C. 2118.

WAR DIARY
or
INTELLIGENCE SUMMARY.
(Erase heading not required.)

Ref. Map. Sheet 37. 1/40.000.

Z 6

Place	Date	Hour	Summary of Events and Information	Remarks and references to Appendices
LANNOY	1.11.18		Coy training in morning. Games in afternoon.	See B (2)
	2.11.18		- do - 9/Lt. W.G. LINDSAY & 2/Lt. MAHONEY joined.	
	3.11.18		Church Parade by 2.0.3. Coys.	
	4.11.18		Baths for No:3 Coy & H.Q. No. 1 & 3 Coys. Coy training in morning. Games in afternoon.	
	5.11.18		" 2 " " - do -	
	6.11.18		" 1 " . Remainder in billets (wet).	
	7.11.18		Coy training in morning 900 to 1230.	
	8.11.18		- do - . No. 1 Coy had 2 platoons repairing shell holes in road from PECQ to WARCOING & debris off road in PECQ. (night)	
	9.11.18		No. 1 Coy working. No. 3 Coy 1st shift on ramp to bridge (being erected by R.E) at PECQ. I.2.a.3.3. No. 2 Coy second shift. Ramp completed & required depth and breadth. Sides require slopings.	
	10.11.18		No. 2 Coy completed Ramp at PECQ BRIDGE. No. 1 Coy repairing road from ESTAMBOURG through PECQ to WARCOING. No. 3 Coy repairing roads to bridge heads at WARCOING & taking in cables at C.21.d.10. I.3.a.9.4. I.b.a.5.5. C.27.b.5.8. No.s 2 & 3 Coys moved to HERINNES.	
	11.11.18		No. 2 Coy repairing craters in PECQ RIVAGE Road. No. 3 Coy repairing WARCOING - HERINNES RIVAGE Road. No. 1 Coy carried on 3 Coys work at 1300. Telegram received from 40th Div Station - Hostilities would cease 1100 11.11.18 No. 1 Coy 2 platoons sawn as 11.11.18. 2 platoons	
	12.11.18		No. 2 Coy same as 11.11.18. No. 3 Coy same as 11.11.18. No. 1 Coy clearing debris from road in PECQ.	
	13.11.18		No. 1 Coy billets. No. 2 & 3 Coys same as 12.11.18.	
	14.11.18		No. 1 Coy Rifles. No. 2 Coy baths. No. 3 Coy same as 12.11.18.	

D. D. & L., London, B.C. (38004) Wt. W1771/M2/31 750,000 5/17 Sch. 52 Forms/C2118/14

Army Form C. 2118.

WAR DIARY
or
INTELLIGENCE SUMMARY.

Ref Map. Sheet 37. 1/40.000.

(Erase heading not required.)

Instructions regarding War Diaries and Intelligence Summaries are contained in F. S. Regs., Part II. and the Staff Manual respectively. Title pages will be prepared in manuscript.

Place	Date	Hour	Summary of Events and Information	Remarks and references to Appendices
LANNOY.	15.11.18.		No. 1. Coy. musketry on Rifle Range nr. ROUBAIX. No. 2. Coy. cont. mused 3 Coy work. No. 3 Coy. ¾ moved from HERINNES to LANNOY.	
"	16.11.18.		No. 1. Coy. training in musketry. No. 2. Coy. completed crackers on PECQ RIVAGE & WARCOING HERINNES moved. No. 3. Coy. baths.	
"	17.11.18.		Special thanksgiving Services held. 3 Officers & O.R. attend 2nd Army Service at ROUBAIX. 1 Officer 50 O.R. attended Divl. Service at LANNOY. Remainder of Battn. less 2 Coy. & R.C. attended Bn. Service at LANNOY. R.C. attended Service at LANNOY church.	
"	18.11.18.		No. 1 Coy. Training. No. 3. musketry on R.R. nr. ROUBAIX. No. 2. Coy. refit.	
"	19.11.18.		No. 1. & 2. Coy. training. No. 3. Coy. refit.	
"	20.11.18 1030		Drill & training in musketry. 0900-1230. Afternoon Sports. Education scheme commenced. classes held in French. Shorthand. Woodwork + Shoemaking. Lectures given on Demobilisation and matters of interest in coming general election. Sundays church Parades.	
			Drafts from Base. 2 Offr. 16 O/Lt. S.MAHONEY, 2/Lt W.G. " " hosp. 6. LINDSAY joined.	
			Strength at beginning of month Offrs. 32 O.R. 703	
			end " " 34 683	
			Casualties. Killed - -	
			Wounded - - 41	
			Evac. Sick - -	
			Other Causes	

W Meiris
Lt. Col.
Comdg. 17th WORC. R. (P)

Army Form C. 2118.

17th Worc Regt (T)

26a

WAR DIARY
or
INTELLIGENCE SUMMARY.
(Erase heading not required.)

Instructions regarding War Diaries and Intelligence Summaries are contained in F. S. Regs., Part II. and the Staff Manual respectively. Title pages will be prepared in manuscript.

Place	Date	Hour	Summary of Events and Information	Remarks and references to Appendices
LANNOY.	1.12.18		Coy training in morning. Games in afternoon.	
	2.12.18		-do- Batt beat Div HQ at football in final round of Div Cup	
	3.12.18		-do- No.2 Coy moved from HERINNES to LANNOY.	
	4.12.18		-do- No.2 Coy beat Batt at football in second round of Div. Cup.	
	5.12.18		-do- M.T. Coy beat Batt at football.	
	6.12.18		-do-	
	8.12.18		Church parade on Sunday. Medal presentation on Sunday afternoon in LANNOY square. Detachment of 6 offrs. 130. O.R. attended.	
	9.12.18		Practice Divisional parade at NECHIN. Battalion attached to 121 Bde for this parade. 2 platoons No.1 Coy at R.E. dump WAMBRECHIES cutting timber for firewood and making billets.	
	10.12.18			
	11.12.18		Coy training in morning.	
	12.12.18		-do-. Divisional cross country run held. The Batt team came in 3rd.	
	13.12.18		Church Parade in cirque Hiodée Roubaix - after service Batt marched past the Divisional Commander.	
	14.12.18		Day spent in cleaning up for inspection.	
	15.12.18		The Batt attended divisional ceremonial parade which was inspected by G.O.C. XV Corps. Lt. Genl. SIR BEAUVOIR DE LISLE. K.C.B. D.S.O. at NECHIN.	
	16.12.18			
	17.12.18 to 21.12.18		Coy parade in morning. P.T. & B.F. close order drill etc. Games in afternoon. Education classes in French. Woodwork. Shorthand held. Up to 21.12.18. 41 Coal miners have been sent to England for demobilisation. Riding classes for officers commenced under 2/Lt FAWCETT. M.M.	
	22.12.18		Church Parade.	

Army Form C. 2118.

WAR DIARY
or
INTELLIGENCE SUMMARY.
(Erase heading not required.)

Instructions regarding War Diaries and Intelligence Summaries are contained in F.S. Regs., Part II. and the Staff Manual respectively. Title pages will be prepared in manuscript.

Place	Date	Hour	Summary of Events and Information	Remarks and references to Appendices
LANNOY	23.12.18		Nos 2 & 3. Coys training 0900-1230. Remainder of 1 Coy moved from LEERS NORD to WAMBRECHIES for work at R.E. dumps.	
	24.12.18		2 & 3. Coys training. No 1. returning new billets	
	25.12.18		Church Parade 1100. Holiday.	
	26.12.18			
	27-30.12.18		Training in morning. Games in afternoon. No 1. Coy working at R.E. dump. WAMBRECHIES.	
	31.12.18		General Survey. MONTH OF DECEMBER. Education scheme has been carried on. Classes to officers in riding have been held. 49 men mostly coal miners have been sent to England for demob. 15 O.R.m. Lectures have been given on Re-enlistment & Demobilisation. Parties of officers and men have attended lectures arranged by Division on various subjects. 64981 Sgt J.W. WILSON awarded French CROIX DE GUERRE de Regiment. Lt. G.A. DIXON, formerly 12. York. R. mentioned in NEW YEARS HONOURS DESPATCH 1919. Off. O.R. 2/Lt DONALDSON evac. to England (sick). Strength at beginning of month. 35. 676. End. 34. 622. Casualties. Evac. Sick. 1. 11. To England for demobilisation 49. Other Causes. - 5. Drafts Received from Hosp. 12. Describes regained. 1. 1.65 13.

Alex Leicef Lt. Col.
Comdg 17 Worc. R. (?)

1.2.19.

Headquarters "A"
40th Division

Herewith War Diary for
this Battalion for the month
of January.

W. Sheppard Major.
Cmmdg. 17th Bn Worcester R
(Pioneers)

WAR DIARY or INTELLIGENCE SUMMARY

Army Form C. 2118.

1st Bn. WORCESTER REGT. (P.H.B.E.)

January 1919.

Place	Date	Hour	Summary of Events and Information	Remarks and references to Appendices
LANNOY	1.1.19		c/o 2 & 3 coys Cross Country run. No 1 coy at WAMBRECHIES shoots. 3 men proceeded to Drill oct in morning. Football in afternoon. 4 men proceeded to V Army Lewis Camp.	
	2.1.19		c/o 2 coy training in morning. c/to 3 coy refreshing Civilian Rifle Range at ROUBAIX	"
	3.1.19		No 2 coy " " " No 3 " " " "	"
	4.1.19		Church parade in our cinema room.	
	5.1.19		Training in morning. 3 men proceeded to V Army Lewis Gun Camp	
	6.1.19		Battalion morning. C/to 2 coy on range in afternoon. Early went to BRUSSELS for 2 day	
	7.1.19		c/o 1 coy on range in morning. 6 pts to 8 Officers riding class in afternoon.	
	8.1.19		P.T. & B.T. training in morning. 6 pts to 8 Officers riding class in afternoon.	
	9.1.19		Drill etc in morning. Coys returned from BRUSSELS one day late owing to engine trouble of train. 4 men attached to Demobilisation Camp	
	10.1.19		47 men proceeded to the 18th (BATTALION) AT LINSELLES	
	11.1.19		2/Lt COX & 2/Lt WAGGOTT & 11 men proceeded to V Army Lewis Gun Camp ST ANDRE.	
	12.1.19		Church parade in morning. 2 " " "	
	13.1.19		Training in morning 3 " " "	
	14.1.19		Batty training & sports.	
	15.1.19		Training & sports.	
	16.1.19		" "	
	17.1.19		Practised for parade to receive Colours	
	18.1.19		2/Lt COL. H.W. BUCHAR D.S.O. to the 11 CCS. 7 men proceeded to demob. Gun Camp	
	19.1.19		Church parade in morning. 6 " " "	
	20.1.19		Final practice parade for receipt of Colours 23 " " "	
	21.1.19		Lt TAYLOR & 18 men proceeded to Demob Gun Camp	
	22.1.19		Rec'd Colours at hand of LT GEN SIR BEAUVOIR DE LISLE K.C.B D.S.O Comdg. XV Corps.	
	23.1.19		25 men proceeded to Demob Gun Camp.	
			No 3 Coy landed in Mobilisation Stores & Bath. Stove	
	24.1.19		No 2 " " " " "	
			Signalling Classes handed in to Bath Stove.	

Army Form C. 2118.

WAR DIARY
or
INTELLIGENCE SUMMARY.
(Erase heading not required.)

Instructions regarding War Diaries and Intelligence Summaries are contained in F. S. Regs., Part II. and the Staff Manual respectively. Title pages will be prepared in manuscript.

Place	Date	Hour	Summary of Events and Information	Remarks and references to Appendices
LANNOY	23-1-19		No 2 Coy handed in Mobilization Stores to Battalion Stores & was proceeded to V Army Demobilization Concentration Camp at St ANDRE.	
	24-1-19		" " " " " " " " " " " " " " " "	
	27-1-19		" " " " " " " " " " " " " " " "	
	28-1-19		" " " " " " " " " " " " " " " "	
			HQ, Lewis & 20 men " " " " " " " " " "	
			Coy working parties strength down to 21, 9 & 27 ranks respectively. Classification of Transport Animals carried out.	
	29-1-19		Pvt. Buck & Pvt Lindsay & 30 men proceeded to St ANDRE for demobilization.	
			No. 1 Coy returned to Battalion for WAMBRECHIES	
	30-1-19		No. 1 Coy handed in Mobilization Stores to Battalion Stores	
			No. 3 Coy taken over from Capt. Cowley-Mcy Major L. M. Southey.	
	31-1-19		En. on fall to much 30 men for working parties.	
			General.	
			During the MONTH of JANUARY Education has gradually come to a close owing to progress of demobilisation.	
			New Year Honours.	
			CAPT. T.K.G. RIDLEY awarded M.C. and GQ.M.S. FEATHERSTONE A.E. & SGT J. SPAYNE awarded M.S.M. (No. 648859)	
			Foreign Honours.	
			LT. COL. H.W. BICHIE D.S.O., C.S.M. ARMSTRONG A. & CPL. D. BIRKINSHAW awarded CROIX-DE-GUERRE of Belgium. (No. 64344) (No. 64011)	
			STRENGTH.	
			Total decrease during month = 8 Officer, 242 other ranks.	

A Shepperd Major.
Comdg. 17th Bn Worcester Regt.
(Pioneers)

A.G.
17th 4th Div

Herewith WAR DIARY for the month
of FEBRUARY.

[Stamp: 17TH BN., WORCESTERSHIRE REGIMENT. No. .... Date 1.3.19]

H.H. Sheppard
Lt. Cl.
Cmdg. 17. Worc. R.

Army Form C. 2118.

WAR DIARY
or
INTELLIGENCE SUMMARY.
(Erase heading not required.)

1/8" WORC R. (2)

Place	Date	Hour	Summary of Events and Information	Remarks and references to Appendices
LANNOY	1.2.19		CAPT. W.N. CROSBY M.C. 2/LT. W SHEPPARD & 8 men proceeded to Demob. Bn. Camp. ST ANDRÉ.	App. B. (2)
	2.2.19		13 Horses sent to Animal Demobilisation Camp at TOURCOING. (not accepted).	
	3.2.19		2/LT. J.S. SMITH & 11 men proceeded to 5 Army Demob. Bn. Camp. ST ANDRÉ.	
	4.2.19		14 men proceeded " " " " "	
	5.2.19		No demobilisation.	
	6.2.19		"	
	7.2.19		Lt. H. TOLSON and 12 men proceeded for demobilisation.	
	8.2.19		9 men proceeded to 5 A.S.B.S. for demobilisation.	28
	9.2.19		Capt Thomas & 8 men proceed for demobilisation	
	10.2.19		7 men proceeded to demobilisation	
	11.2.19		– No demobilisation.	
	12.2.19		22. OR. proceeded for demobilisation	
	13.2.19		17 OR. – do –	
	14.2.19		10 OR. – do –	
	15.2.19		10 OR. orders received that Bn will proceed to DIEPPE & demob all retainable personnel of 2nd Bn. WORC. R. all detailed personnel recalled.	
	16.2.19		5 OR. proceeded for demobilisation.	
	17.2.19		5 OR. – do –	
	18.2.19		No demobilisation	
	19.2.19		– do – Lt. Col. H.W. BECHER. D.S.O. evacuated to England. (sick).	
	20.2.19		2 men proceed for demobilisation 2/Lt. S.T. HUMPHRIES demob England to join WORC. R. depot.	
	21.2.19		14 " " " " 2/LT. W.H. FAWCETT M.M. to England to join MANCH. R. depot	
	22.2.19		1 man " " " – 2/LT. W. SHRIMPTON & 2/LT A.G. HOLLAND demobilized on leave.	
	23.2.19		No demobilisation.	

17. **WORCESTERSHIRE R.** WAR DIARY or INTELLIGENCE SUMMARY.

Army Form C. 2118.

Place	Date	Hour	Summary of Events and Information	Remarks and references to Appendices
Lannoy.	24.2.19		No demobilisation.	
"	25.2.19		- do -	
"	26.2.19		- do -	
	27.2.19		1 O.R. proceeded to concentration Camp for demobilisation	
	28.2.19		do	
			General Strength at beginning of month. Offrs 27, O.R. 383. End " 16, " 202. 10 officers demobilised Lt.Col. Iw. BECHER to England (sick)	
			172 O.R. demobilised (includes those demobilised whilst on leave). 11 S.O.S. evac. to hosp. sick	
			14 men have re-enlisted under A.O.4. of Dec. 1918.	
			4 officers & 2 O.R. have volunteered for Army of occupation as laid down in A.O. XIV d/29.1.19.	
			Personnel for Battalion Cadre have been selected.	
			AWARDS. The following N.C.O.s have been awarded the MILITARY MEDAL for devotion to duty & good work carried out for period Sept 17 to Nov. 11. 1918 Sgt GOODRUM. 64592 L.C. PARKINSON. 64892. Sgt GILLESPIE. 64030. Sgt BUTTALL. 64897	

HWShepperd Lt Col.
Comdg. 17. Worc. R.(P.)

Z 8

R.P.C.
3rd Echelon

Herewith WAR DIARY for 17. Worc R/R
for month of MARCH 1919.

[Stamp: 17th BN., WORCESTERSHIRE REGIMENT. No. ... Date 2.4.19]

H.P. Sheppard Col.
Cmdg. 17. Worc R.

Army Form C. 2118.

40

17 Worc R P

Vol 9 40

Z 9

WAR DIARY or INTELLIGENCE SUMMARY.

(Erase heading not required.)

WORCESTERSHIRE REGIMENT.

Instructions regarding War Diaries and Intelligence Summaries are contained in F.S. Regs., Part II. and the Staff Manual respectively. Title pages will be prepared in manuscript.

Place	Date	Hour	Summary of Events and Information	Remarks and references to Appendices
TANNOY	1.3.19		3 O.R. proceeded to demobilisation Camp ST ANDRE for demobilisation.	
"	2.3.19		7 O.R. do	
"	3.3.19		11 O.R. do	
"	4.3.19		No demobilisation.	
"	5.3.19		5 officers (Lt A MARDER. 2/Lieuts W MAHONEY D.C.M. C.F. WALLER. A.J. SMART & J.A. BURGOYNE) & 61 other Ranks transferred to 2/8 WORC R. 615 Do 25 O.R. at present on leave posted to 2/8 WORC R.	
"	6.3.19		No demobilisation.	
"	7.3.19		- do -	
"	8.2.19		- do -	
"	9.3.19		16 OR proceeded to Demobilisation Camp ST ANDRE for demobilisation.	
"	10.3.19		No demobilisation the Battn has only 9 O.R. eligible for demobilisation present with unit.	
"	11.3.19		No demobilisation. 17 Animals evacuated to horse attaching Camp TOURCOING.	
"	-20.3.19		On 17.3.19. Bn Cadre paraded w.lt 12 Bdr at TOUFFLERS for General Sir W. E. PEYTON K.C.B. K.C.V.O. D.S.O. G.O.C. 40th Division to wish all ranks good luck and to say good bye	
"	21.3.19		No demobilisation.	
"	22.3.19		4 O.R. proceeded to demobilisation Camp ST AUDY for demobilisation. The Cadre entrained at CROIX at 1500 hours for HAVRE & pole own material for send of 2/1 WORC R. on journey to HAVRE.	
HAVRE	23.3.19		Arrived HAVRE 1500 hours & proceeded to billets in CINDER CITY CAMP HAVRE on order of Worc R. the Battalion is now administered by 33rd Division.	

Army Form C. 2118.

WAR DIARY
or
INTELLIGENCE SUMMARY.

17' WORC. R.

(Erase heading not required.)

Instructions regarding War Diaries and Intelligence Summaries are contained in F. S. Regs., Part II. and the Staff Manual respectively. Title pages will be prepared in manuscript.

Place	Date	Hour	Summary of Events and Information	Remarks and references to Appendices
CONDÉ R.CNY CAMP. HAVRE	30.3.19 31.3.19		B⁹ Codes cleaning up. General. Strength at beginning of month off. OR 16. 202. End. — 8. 69* * includes 25 OR on leave S off & 81 OR transferred to 2/5 WORO R. Lieut & Qu. 3 MULHALL transferred to 16.4.19. 9/17 WADDUP & 9/17 PERKINS demobilised. 42 other Ranks demobilised during the month 5 other Ranks demobilised whilst on leave. 1 man re-enlisted under A.O. 4 of Dec. 1918. Awards. 64750. Sergt T. MUGGERIDGE awarded the following BELGIAN decorations — CHEVALIER de L'ORDRE de LEOPOLD II and CROIX de GUERRE	

H.E.Appurdt Cr.
Comdg. 17. Wor. R.

WAR DIARY
or
INTELLIGENCE SUMMARY.

Army Form C. 2118.

May – Oct 1919

17th Bn Worcestershire Regt

Place	Date	Hour	Summary of Events and Information	Remarks and references to Appendices
GINZER	1st May		Routine duties. Beach and Harbour Guard. The Company at Ginzer Camp.	
CITY	2			
CAMP	3			
LE HAVRE	4			
	5		2/Lt W. Shaw to 17th Bn WR. 2/Lt W.H.P. Hope MC 2/Lt J.R. Cooley S/Staff Capt Jones as a posting from 1/5 P.O. Staff Regt.	
	6		2/Lt C.B. Jones and 2/Lt B. Young MC P&O Staff Regt. join Bn on posting from 1/5 P.O. Staff Regt.	
	7		Routine duties. Guard and one Company at Greenery.	
	8		One platoon other ranks posted to Bn from Havre 7 PB	
	9		Routine duties. Guard and one Company at Greenery	
	10			
	11			
	12		2/Lt R. Jones & 2/Lt Jackson posting from 1/5 P.O. Staff Regt. 2/Lt E.W. Potter MC joins from 3rd Bn	
	13		Routine duties. Guard and one Company at Greenery	
	14			
	15			

Z 10

Army Form C. 2118.

WAR DIARY
or
INTELLIGENCE SUMMARY.
(Erase heading not required.)

17th Bn Northumberland Regt

Place	Date 1919	Hour	Summary of Events and Information	Remarks and references to Appendices
CINDER CITY	17 May		Lt E H Duffield M.C. posted to No 255 P.O.W. Coy for duty	
	18		Route March. Guard & one Company at Kenty.	
	19		Inspection of Bn Transport by the Brigadier General.	
	20		Routine duties, guard & one Company at Kenty.	
LE HAVRE	21			
	22			
	23			
	24		Lt Col Holding 3? Manchester Regt, Lt O. T. Corbett 16th D.L.I. Lt. & Qrme Griffith, 2nd/Lieut Fowler, & 2nd/Lt Irecave M.C. & Q.(a) & Capt Jones OBE on posting from 51st Bn D.L.I.	
	25			
	26			
	27		Routine duties. Guard and 1 Company at Kenty.	
	28			
	29			
	30			
	31			

Bn Strength
1st May 1919, 37 Officers 949 other Ranks
31st May 1919 today " 9 + 3 "

J.J. Beecham Lt Col
C.O. 17th Bn N'bre Regt

Army Form C. 2118.

17 Worcester Vol 12

WAR DIARY
or
INTELLIGENCE SUMMARY.
(Erase heading not required.)

Z 11

Place	Date 1919	Hour	Summary of Events and Information	Remarks and references to Appendices
Cairo City Citadel	1st June		The Cadre of the 2nd Bn having been ordered to parade today, an escort of 4 officers & 100 other ranks under Capt. C.F. de C. Ethrington paraded at 12.30 hrs to escort the Colours of the 2nd Bn to the Docks. The Cadre, Escort and Band of 100th Brigade were formed up on parade with massed Colours under the Command of Lt. Col. J.H. Bonney DSO. Accompanied by the Brig. General Guggisberg C.M.G., DSO, Commanding 100th Brigade who afterwards advanced the Cadre. The parade then moved past acknowledging the march to the Docks where the Escort formed into line. The Colours were then marched off to the S.S. Spondorosberg where the Escort presented arms the Band played the King.	
	2			
	3		Lieut. Brien, 13th Yorks, joined Bn. on posting from 52nd Div.	Divine Service
	4		Lieut. Rattage 6th Essex joined Bn. on posting from 42nd Div.	Guards
	5			and Training
	6			
	7		Lieut. Laurence 4/5 Hapt. joined Bn. on posting from Aldershot.	
	8			
	9			
	10			
	11			

Army Form C. 2118

WAR DIARY
or
INTELLIGENCE SUMMARY.
(Erase heading not required.)

17th Bn. Worcestershire R.

Place	Date	Hour	Summary of Events and Information	Remarks and references to Appendices
No 91 Camp	12 June 1919		The Battn moved from Cinder City Camp to No 91 new Camp: No 21 Camp Harfleur.	
	13		Commdg Officer inspected the Camp.	
Harfleur	14		Bn & Rhoda Hunt company formed. Divine Service. Battalion Parade 10:15.	
	15			
	16		Usual am. Duties. Guards. Training	
	17			
	18			
	19		Lieut & Qr Mr C. Rodes 12th York & Lanc Regt. joins Bn for Duty. } Routine duties
	20		} for Training
	21		Divine Service. Battn Parade 10:15.	
	22		Inspection of Camp by Divisional Commdr. Major Gen. J. Duncan CB Cmg DSO.	
	23		Battn holding a Thanksgiving service held on account of Germans accepting Peace Terms	
	24			
	25			
	26		Lieut D Kelly MC attached 'B' Group ? to England. 2/Lt S.C. Young, 2/Lt J.E. Daly, 2/Lt J.C. Coley and 2/Lt ... proceed to Dieppe superintending Battn at Base Sports	
	27			
	28		Guards. Ordinary Drills. Training	
	29		Peace Celebrated in town. Men given leave facilities to visit town.	
	30		Divine Service. Battn Parade 09:45 hrs. Temporary Battn orders normally issued by 16 KORLC in order to allow of Battn being orders out. That Guards practising Battn Ceremony.	

Battn Strength & Return
1st June 1919 — 44 Officers 943 other ranks
30th June 1919 — 44 Officers 903 other ranks

J. Weathers
Lt Colonel
Commdg 17th Bn Worc. Regt.

Army Form C. 2118

WAR DIARY
or
INTELLIGENCE SUMMARY. 1/7th Bn Worcestershire Regt
(Erase heading not required.) Vol 13

Z/12

Place	Date 1919	Hour	Summary of Events and Information	Remarks and references to Appendices
No 21 Camp HARFLEUR	1 July		Route duties, Garrison Guards, one Company at Training.	
	2		16th Royal Scots on an Garrison Guard found by the Battn. Battalion Ceremonial Parade.	
	3		The 100th Infantry Brigade paraded for a Review by Brig Gen H. Guggisberg, C.M.G., D.S.O. C.in C. of the Brigade. In consequence of Thanksgiving Service for Peace was held at the conclusion of the Review. The Bay. Gen afterwards expressed himself as exceptionally pleased with the General turn out, steadiness and discipline of the Bat on Parade.	
	4			
	5			
	6			
	7		Route duties, Garrison Guards, one ne Company at training.	
	8			
	9			
	10			
	11			
	12		Battalion Sports were held. Lieut A.F. Webb posted to 163 P.O.W. Coy. Divn Service Barrels.	
	13			

Army Form C. 2118.

WAR DIARY
or
INTELLIGENCE SUMMARY.
(Erase heading not required.)

17th Bn. Nottinghamshire Regt.

Place	Date	Hour	Summary of Events and Information	Remarks and references to Appendices
No 21 Camp HARFLEUR	1919 19th July		French National Fête and Peace Celebration. A corporate party of 6 Officers and 137 Other ranks with the Colours found No 3 Company of a British Composite Battalion under the command of the 61st P. Inspn D Co. 2nd Lancashire Regt. who took part in a review in the town of HAVRE, held by the Armed Governor on Havre. Congratulations were received from the GOC 61st Division, the 100th Infy Bde, & the Naval Officer in command at Havre, on the turn out, marches, and fine bearing of the Company. Commanders were also received from the Armed Governor on Havre, thanking the Bne Commander, expressing the gratitude of the people of Havre for the part taken by the British on this solemn Fête & festive celebration, a July 14th were stating that the orderly heavy, smart turn out, splendid marches of the Company were the subject of favourable comment by the French heard military Officers, & a source of respect & pride to the R. Regt. & General Liddell in command	

Army Form C. 2118

WAR DIARY
INTELLIGENCE SUMMARY.
(Erase heading not required.)

1/7 Bn Worcestershire Regt

Vol 13

Place	Date	Hour	Summary of Events and Information	Remarks and references to Appendices
No 21 Camp HARFLEUR	July 1919 1.		Routine duties. Guard, Guard, One Company at Training	
	2.		16th Regt. turned out all Guards Guards found by 16 Bn	
	3.		Battn. Ceremonial Parade.	
	4.		The 100th Infantry Brigade turned for a Review by Brig. E.R. Huggeting, G.O.C. 100 Coy of the Brigade. 2nd Rumbogong Service was for Peace was held at the conclusion of the Review. The Brig. gave afternoon experience enough a exceptionally fine roll the General turnout, steadiness and discipline of the men on Parade.	
	5. 6.		Routine duties, Guards, Guards, one one Company at Training.	
	7.			
	10-13		Battalion Sports were held. Lieut A.R. Lillith posted to 163 P.O.W. Coy. Divine Service Parade.	

Army Form C. 2118.

WAR DIARY
or
INTELLIGENCE SUMMARY.
(Erase heading not required.)

17th Bn. Worcestershire Regt.

Place	Date	Hour	Summary of Events and Information	Remarks and references to Appendices
No 21 Camp HARFLEUR	1919 14 July		French National Fête and Peace Celebration. A composite Company of 6 Officers, and 137 other ranks with the Colours found by Company of a British Composite Battalion, near the No 3 Company of 7th Bn Pt. Supf. D Co. 2nd Lancashire Regt. this Regt. & the 4th R. Sussex Regt. took part in a review in the town of HAVRE, led by the Armed Governor on Horse. Congratulations were received from the G.O.C. 61st Division, G.O.C. 100th Infy Bde., & the Naval Officer in Command at Havre, on the turn out, smartness, and fine bearing of the Company. A Commendation was also received from the Armed Governor of Havre, through the Base Commander, expressing the gratitude of the people of Havre for the part taken by the British in the National Fête. During Celebration a Jazz Band was also one of the Orderly keeping small band and Bandsmen also some of the Company were the object of special comment by the General, and Military Officer, & a source of special pride to the R. Regt. of gratified thanks on this occasion	

Army Form C. 2118.

WAR DIARY
or
INTELLIGENCE SUMMARY.
(Erase heading not required.)

17th Bn Worcestershire Regt

Place	Date 1919	Hour	Summary of Events and Information	Remarks and references to Appendices
No 21 Camp 15th July HARFLEUR	16th		"A" Coy reported Hd Qrs Feer. P.O.W. Depot Lauenville	
	17th		The 19th Sutnor stopped as a Guard Kiting to Cancelor	
	18th		with the Peace Celebrations held in England.	
	19th		The Battalion was other carrying out normal	
	20th		undergo a course of training. From the 16th July to	
	21st			
	22nd		the 26th July or Drue and Infantry	
	23rd			
	24th		Instruction for wearing the ribbon of the British War Medal	
	25th		1914-1919 — were received on the 23rd inst, and the ribbon were	
	26th		at once	
	27th		Issued for Wespor bished to 17th Gloucesters Rgt on 23rd Inst.	
	28th			
	29th		Routine duties Garrison Guard, Ore Company at Treveny	
	30th		Libereton Company of 16th KRRC at P.O.W. Depot Lauenville	
	31st		6 Bn Strength Return	

1st July 1919. 44 Officers 907 Rank
31st July 1919 45 Officers 832 Rank

J.A. Buckman Lieut Col
Comdg 17th Bn Worcestershire Regt

Army Form C. 2118.

WAR DIARY
or
INTELLIGENCE SUMMARY.
(Erase heading not required.)

17th Bn. Worcestershire Regt.

Z.13

Place	Date	Hour	Summary of Events and Information	Remarks and references to Appendices
HARFLEUR No. 21 CAMP	1918 Aug 1		Routine duties, games, games, and one company at Docks	
	2			
	3			
	4			
	5			
	6		The Bn fire part in a Review hour of the 10th Infantry Brigade on the Parade ground of the old Infantry Base Depot to meet good bye to Brig Gen G.G. Guggisberg C.M.G. D.S.O who was going up to command of the Brigade. Lieut Col J.F. Barker D.S.O. now in command of the Parade. The Brigade afterwards marched the Brigade and expressed to the appreciation of the Honours and what the old been the ones and their interest taken in command of the Brigade, of of the state of efficiency which had been attained.	
	7		Routine duties, games, games and one company at	
	8			
	9			
	10			
	11			
	12			

Army Form C. 2118.

Sheet IV

WAR DIARY
or
INTELLIGENCE SUMMARY.

17th Bn. Worcestershire Regt.

(Erase heading not required.)

Instructions regarding War Diaries and Intelligence Summaries are contained in F. S. Regs., Part II. and the Staff Manual respectively. Title pages will be prepared in manuscript.

Place	Date 1919	Hour	Summary of Events and Information	Remarks and references to Appendices
HARFLEUR No 21 CAMP	Aug 13 14 15 16 17 18 19		Return duties, games, games and ordinary not company or Parades	
	20 21 22 23		Orders were received that all ordinary work given the colours under Lord Derby's Scheme for returnes since before 1st July 1916, were to be eligible for demobilisation. Return duties etc Went forward parades for dispersal Routine duties etc	
	24 25 26 27 28 29 30 31		32 other ranks proceed for dispersal 38 other ranks proceed for dispersal 9 other ranks proceed for dispersal Routine duties etc 11th Bal. Gone over to Transit Camp 6 Parade State.	1st Aug 19. Off 45 OR 833. 31st Aug 19. Off 42 OR 747.

J. Buckham Lieut Col
Comd 17/Bn Worcestershire Regt

Army Form C. 2118.

WAR DIARY
or
INTELLIGENCE SUMMARY.
(Erase heading not required.)

17th Bn. Somerset Light Inf.

Z/14

Place	Date 1919	Hour	Summary of Events and Information	Remarks and references to Appendices
No 31 Camp Harfleur	1st Sept		Orders were received for 15 Officers and 300 Other Ranks to proceed to Dunkirk to act as escort to German Prisoners of war being repatriated to Germany. 3 Officers & 150 Other Ranks to escort every 100 German POWs then to be taken prisoner to Germany.	
	2nd		Routine duties	
	3rd			
	4th			
	5th			
	6th			
	7th			
	8th			
	9th			
	10th			
	11th			
	12th		LCI No 639 authorizing the wearing of the Khaki beret Ribbon was received.	
	13th			

Army Form C. 2118.

WAR DIARY
or
INTELLIGENCE SUMMARY.
(Erase heading not required.)

Instructions regarding War Diaries and Intelligence Summaries are contained in F. S. Regs., Part II. and the Staff Manual respectively. Title pages will be prepared in manuscript.

Place	Date	Hour	Summary of Events and Information	Remarks and references to Appendices
N° 91 Camp Honfleur	1919 April 15th 16th		Officer were received as they of new on to from the camp yesterday as under the Derby Area The following officers Capt Grant M.C. R.F.A. Bucarne to Nylon Capt L. Cabot, 2/Lt R Joseph, 2/Lt A R Nylon M.C., 2/Lt J R Cosley are 2/Lt J.C. Howard proceed to depose	17th By Buckinghamshire Reg
	17th		Lieut J.P. Jones to the town, It 12.00 hought 2/Lt R.A. were on to the home proceed to depose. Lieut Col A.S Henry D.S.O assumed command of the Battalion vice Lieut Col J.P. Baker D.S.O about to England	
	18th		78/64 other ranks proceed to defence The following officers were posted and proceed to you onto defence 2/Lt A.F. Hotchey to 1/4 Labour Coy Lieut R.J. Rocks proceed Lieut A.F. Howard to 3/4 Infantry Labour Lieut B.E Cox 2/C proceed for defence	

Army Form C. 2118.

WAR DIARY
INTELLIGENCE SUMMARY
(Erase heading not required.)

17th Bn. Worcestershire Regiment

Place	Date	Hour	Summary of Events and Information	Remarks and references to Appendices
No 2.I. Camp Kantara	1919 19th Sept.		by Order Ranks proceeded for disposal. 2/m. J.L. Edwards proceeded for disposal.	
	20 Oct		73 other Ranks proceeded for disposal.	
	21 Oct		Capt. H.E. Boswell D.S.O. M.C. assumed the duties of Adjutant to the Bn. vice Captain C.C. Dargh M.C. ordered to England to join the 2nd Battalion. The Worcestershire Regiment. Warning order received for Bn. to move to No. 2. Rest Camp.	
	22.9		54 Other Ranks proceeded for disposal.	
	23rd		7/m. W.C. Ebon proceeded for disposal. 25 Other Ranks proceeded for disposal.	
	24th		War Office Wire received cancelling Egyptian Draft authority D. 35d 92 to dilute 17th inst.	

Army Form C. 2118.

WAR DIARY
INTELLIGENCE SUMMARY.
(Erase heading not required.)

Sheet 4.

Place	Date	Hour	Summary of Events and Information	Remarks and references to Appendices
Alnwick Barracks	1919 Sept 24		6 men proceeded for dispersal	
	25		36 men proceeded for dispersal.	
	26		10 men proceeded for dispersal. Orders received to reduce to cadre forthwith. Cadre received for 8 officers not available released O.R.R. to 9th Bn Northumberland Fusiliers released men to be demobilised forthwith.	
	27		12 men proceeded for dispersal.	
	28		Routine duties	
	29		Lieut Mahon A.I. and 4 other Ranks proceed for dispersal, Ten other ranks attached to Army Postal Service	

Sheet 1.

WAR DIARY
INTELLIGENCE SUMMARY
(Erase heading not required.)

Army Form C. 2118.

17th Bn. Northumberland Regt.

Place	Date 1919	Hour	Summary of Events and Information	Remarks and references to Appendices
No 21 Camp Havre	1st Feb.		Routine Duties. 1 O.R. proceeded for dispersal.	
	2nd		Capt. C.L. de B. Hinds, Lt. H.H.J. Good 2/Lt. D. Gordon M.C. + 40 O.Rs. proceeded to join the 9th Bn. Northumberland Fus.	
	3rd		Capt. K.D. Bell, 2/Lt. J. Barr + 40 O.Rs. proceeded to join the 9th Bn. Northumberland Fus. Lt. W. Loynes, 2/Lt. A. Mellor M.M. 2/Lt. A.S. Wall + 41 O.R. proceeded to join the 9th Bn. Northumberland Fus.	2/15
	5th		Routine Duties.	
	6th		Routine Duties.	

Army Form C. 2118.

WAR DIARY
INTELLIGENCE SUMMARY.
(Erase heading not required.)

17th Bn Worc: Rgt.

Instructions regarding War Diaries and Intelligence Summaries are contained in F. S. Regs., Part II. and the Staff Manual respectively. Title pages will be prepared in manuscript.

Place	Date	Hour	Summary of Events and Information	Remarks and references to Appendices
21 Camp Hangelow	7th Oct.		2. O.Rs. proceeded for disposal.	
	8th Oct.		Equipment Guard proceeded to No. 2 Rest Camp for internation to England. Battalion details of 17th Worc: Rgt. proceeded to No. 2 Rest Camp. The 17th Bn the Worcestershire Regiment ceased to exist. Strength of Battn. 1/10/19. = 23 Officers. & 309 O.Rs. 8/10/19 = Nil. (10th + 13 O.Rs. Equipment Gd.)	

A Stewart
Lieut. Col.
Commdg 17th Bn The Worc: Rgt.

Stray/wo/95/M

www.ingramcontent.com/pod-product-compliance
Lightning Source LLC
Chambersburg PA
CBHW081546160426
43191CB00011B/1856